Introducti

L ying between the Vale of Clwyd and the S
little known wild, beautiful, unspoilt upl
by walkers and tourists alike as they head to crowuou ......
heart is a large undulating upland plateau containing an expansive heather
moorland, now designated Open Access land, and several large lakes, most
notably Llyn Brenig, with its Visitor Centre and nearby Alwen reservoir. On
its eastern side is Clocaenog Forest - an important habitat for red squirrels
– and elsewhere are delightful open hills.

The area has been occupied by man since about 5700 B.C. when a bet-
ter climate and woodland habitat first attracted nomadic hunters. It contains
important Bronze Age ceremonial and burial sites and Iron-Age hillforts.
From the Middle Ages to the 19th century black cattle, often from Anglesey,
were grazed on the upland pastures before being taken by drovers to distant
markets in England. Cerrigydrudion is the largest settlement, lying on an
important drovers route and the original 18thC London–Holyhead turnpike
coach road, later improved by Thomas Telford, now the A5. In 1854, George
Borrow, the eminent traveller and author of *Wild Wales* walked this way.

Easily accessible, the area offers excellent walking with a great sense
of space and superb views, especially of the mountains of Snowdonia from
the western part of the area. The 21 circular walks in this book explore its
moorland, hills, river valleys, lakes, woods and forests. They follow old
drovers' roads and visit ancient communities and sites of historical interest,
whilst providing an insight into the area's history. They include sections of
the waymarked linear Mynydd Hiraethog Trail linking the area's scattered vil-
lages, the popular circuit of Llyn Brenig and the newly created Alwen Trail.

The routes, which range from a 2½ mile archaeological trail to an
exhilarating 10½ mile moorland challenge, follow public rights of way or
permissive paths. A key feature is that most individual routes, as well as
containing shorter walk options, can easily be linked to provide longer and
more challenging day walks, if required. Be suitably equipped, especially
on the more remote exposed moorland routes. Walking boots are recom-
mended, along with appropriate clothing to protect against the elements.
Please remember that the condition of paths can vary according to season
and weather. Refer any path problems encountered to the relevant Highways
Department (*see page 40*).

Each walk has a detailed map and description which enables the route
to be followed without difficulty, but be aware that changes in detail can
occur at any time. The location of each walk is shown on the back cover and
a summary of their key features is also given. This includes an estimated
walking time, but allow more time to enjoy the scenery. Please observe the
country code. *Enjoy your walking!*

WALK I
AFON CLYWEDOG & FOEL GANOL

DESCRIPTION A delightful 4-mile walk exploring the valleys and hills near Cyffylliog – an old community set in the wooded Clywedog valley some 4 miles west of Ruthin – offering extensive views. The route, which is part of a waymarked Mynydd Hiraethog circuit, follows a lovely section of the Clywedog river, then rises up an attractive side valley to follow a high-level country road along the northern slopes of Foel Ganol. It then descends to Cyffylliog by either a delightful open green track, and road (**A**) or by upland pasture (**B**). Allow about 2½ hours. The Red Lion, a traditional village inn offering good food and drink, makes a good finish to the walk.

START Cyffylliog [SJ 060578]

DIRECTIONS From Ruthin take the B55105 towards Cerrigydrudion and just after passing Llanfwrog church, take the road signposted to Cyffylliog. Go through Bontuchel and after crossing the river into Cyffylliog, park tidily on the right opposite the school and cottages

According to folklore, the parish was haunted by mischievous fairies, who used to take horses from their stables and ride them all night, returning them dirty and exhausted. So, it is best to explore this area during daylight hours – just in case!

I From the centre of the village, take the road signposted to Nantglyn. Soon you pass the old Georgian 'hearse house' and medieval Church of St. Mary founded in the 15thC. 100 yards beyond the church, take the signposted path on the right between Hyfrydle and an old barn to cross a footbridge over the Afon Clywedog. Follow the path LEFT, passing beneath a house and on past its access bridge over the river to go through a gate. Now follow a delightful scenic path alongside the river. After crossing a stile by a gate the waymarked path continues a little way from the river, goes through a

gate, crosses a stream, then descends a green access track beneath a cottage. After going through gate, as the track descends to the river, take a path on the right angling away from the track to pass through a short section of forest, soon rising above the fast-flowing river in a more open aspect – *with wind turbines visible above the conifers further down the valley.* The path continues to rise through the edge of the forest, then descends to a signposted green track T-junction. Turn RIGHT up the track and follow it through the forest edge to cross a stile by a gate – *with good views across the Concwest valley.*

2 Here you leave the waymarked trail and go straight ahead on a green track, which climbs steadily up the western slopes of Foel Uchaf to reach a road. Turn RIGHT and follow this attractive quiet upland country road as it contours along the northern slopes of Foel Ganol – *providing steady walking and extensive open views: north towards Denbigh, the northern Clwydians, and the coast at Rhyl; and ahead to the central Clwydian Hills, extending south from Moel y Parc with its TV. transmitter mast to the highest point-Moel Famau, with its distinctive ruined Jubilees Tower – and on to Moel Fenlli, with its Iron-Age hillfort.* After ¾ mile, at a road junction just before an old farm, keep with the right fork, bending south with the road.

3 Here you have a choice of return routes.

For route A continue along the road, then at a cattle-grid, cross a waymarked stile on the left. Now follow the signposted path along a green track across the open upland pasture of Moel y Fron – *with extensive views west.* As the delightful track begins to descend, passing the tiny Llyn Gloyw, new views unfold of the Clwydian hills and the Llantisilio Mountains. Eventually the track ends at a road. Follow the road down into Cyffylliog.

For route B, about 100 yards beyond the farm, take a signposted path over a stile on the right and follow a green track along the field edge parallel with the road. Soon the track descends to a gate and continues down to Foel Ganol cottage. At its far gar-

2

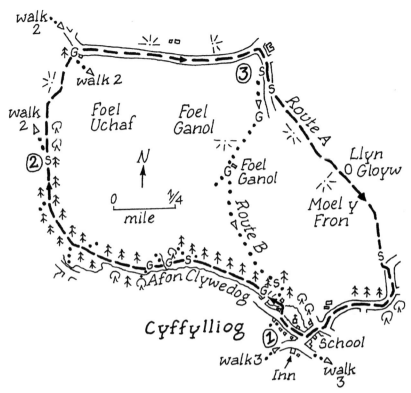

walk 2

walk 2

walk 2

walk 2

Foel Uchaf

Foel Ganol

③

N

0 ¼ mile

Foel Ganol

Route A

Route B

Llyn O Gloyw

Moel y Fron

②

Afon Clywedog

Cyffylliog

School

walk 3

Inn

walk 3

den corner, go through a gate and continue ahead down a large field to go through a waymarked gateway in the bottom corner. Go down the next field, parallel with the tree boundary on your right, and on to cross a stile at the left-hand wood corner. Follow the path down through the trees to pass behind a house and down through the garden edge to join your outward route.)

Hearse House

3

WALK 2

CLYWEDOG RESERVOIR & FOEL UCHAF

DESCRIPTION A 9 mile stretched figure of eight walk (A) featuring attractive wooded river valleys, open hills, forest, a hidden upland reservoir and excellent views. The route also offers an alternative 3¾ (B) or 4½ (C) mile walk around Foel Uchaf. The main walk follows part of a waymarked Mynydd Hiraethog path along the attractive Clywedog and Concwest valleys, before rising steadily on lanes and open/forestry tracks to reach the Clywedog reservoir, lying at over 1300 feet amongst forest. The return route follows a bridleway past the delightful small hill of Bryn Ocyn, currently Tir Gofal permissive access land, which provides an optional extension for views. This is subject to review, so please check its status on CCW's access map (www.ccw.gov.uk) and look for signs on the ground. The route returns to the Concwest valley, then follows an attractive upland road, before crossing Foel Uchaf and making a delightful descent back into the Clywedog valley. Allow about 4½ hours.
START Cyffylliog [SJ 060578] See **Walk 1**.

I Follow instructions for the first section of **Walk 1**.

2 (For **Walk B** continue ahead up the green track. Just before it reaches the road at point 5, turn right along another track and continue with the main described route.) For Walks A and C, go half-LEFT with the way-marked Mynydd Hiraethog path to another stile just ahead. Continue in the same direction along the top field edge, soon through an area of gorse, to reach a waymark post. Here, go half-LEFT through an area of reed and thistle, to cross a stile in a fence corner. Continue ahead alongside a fence and on to follow a path by or near the Afon Concwest, along the bottom edge of a delightful area of predominantly oak woodland. After crossing a stile, keep on by the river, over another

stile, and on to reach a road. (For **Walk C**, turn right and follow the road to point **5**.)

3 Turn LEFT and follow the road up to a junction. Turn RIGHT up the no through road. After a while the lane levels out to pass Bryn-ochan farm. After passing a ruin on your right the road bends to a large house and becomes a track. Continue along the track – *enjoying panoramic views across the Clywedog valley to the Clwydian Hills –* soon gently descending to cross a cattle grid. Keep ahead down the main track, soon bending down through a gate and heading west along the top edge of the Clywedog valley – *with wind turbines above the forest skyline ahead.* When the track splits, go up the right fork. After a gate, follow the stony track as it rises steadily through the forest. *As you get higher, forest clearance provides good*

Clywedog Reservoir

Bryn-o

views of the deep gorge at the narrow head of the valley. After just over a mile you reach the unexpected sight of Clywedog reservoir (private) – *popular with wildfowl and fishermen.*

4 Return along the track, and when it bends right, go up another forestry track on the left. After about 150 yards, take a green track (a bridleway) on the right. Follow it through the open forest to go through a gate into upland pasture. (From here, if still available, a waymarked Tir Gorfal path will take you up to the top of nearby Bryn Ochan for good all-round views.) The main route continues with the green track alongside the fence, past the forest corner and on to cross a stile near the fence corner – *with extensive views of the Clwydian Hills and the distant Berwyns to the south.* Follow the green track across and down the upland pasture towards

4

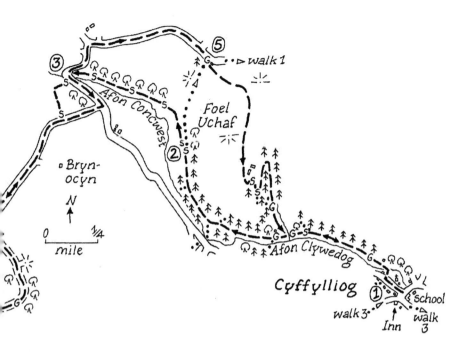

the house passed earlier, over a stile and on with the track, passing through two gates to rejoin your outward route at the road. Follow it back past Bryn-ochan farm. Later cross a stile on the left and head straight down the steep field. At the bottom edge above bracken, a path descends a few yards, then bears RIGHT down to a stile to reach the road at point **3**. Follow the road up to a junction. Turn RIGHT, past a side road, and follow the steadily rising road. *This attractive quiet upland country road with its varied hedgerow flowers is a delight.*

5 After passing another side road, take a signposted path through a gate on your right by a corrugated shed. Follow the track up across the northern slopes of Foel Uchaf. At a prominent viewpoint – *with superb*

views looking north to Denbigh and down the Vale of Clwyd to the coast – the track bends south across Foel Uchaf – *soon offering good views of the Clywedog valley and the southern Clwydian Hills.* Follow the track down, and just after it bends towards a farm, take a signposted path over a stile on the right. Follow the path down between trees and the fence to cross another stile in the corner, then bear LEFT to follow a rough track along the edge of a forest, soon bending RIGHT down through the trees. When the track splits, take the left fork down to a gate at the forest edge. Go down the field towards a cottage, soon alongside a stream on your left, to a small gate to the left of the cottage. Go down its access track, and when it bends right, turn LEFT and simply follow your outward route back to the start.

WALK 3
PINCYN LLYS FROM CYFFYLLIOG

DESCRIPTION A 7-mile walk through undulating upland pasture and forest to the top of Pincyn Llys, with its unusual stone monument and panoramic views. Allow about 3½ hours. A shorter 3¼ mile walk is included.
START Cyffylliog [SJ 060578] See **Walk 1**.

Pincyn Llys is a part-forested hill (1354 feet) lying between Cyffylliog and Clocaenog. The monument was erected in 1830 by the Second Lord Bagot to commemorate the planting of forest. A later inscription records that the plantation was felled during and after the 1914-18 war, and Clocaenog Forest was created in 1930. The monument stands at the corner of an ancient earthwork known as 'Llys y Frenhines' – 'The Queen's Court House' – from which a boulder shaped like an armchair called 'Cader y Frenhines' ('The Queen's Chair') was removed to Lord Bagot's residence at Pool Park in 1804.

I Take the minor road leading east from the Red Lion, past a phone box. Follow it for about 1¼ miles. About 200 yards beyond Tyddyn-Bach, turn RIGHT up a track to cross a stile. Continue up the track, and immediately after it bends left, take a path on the right, which rises steadily along the wood edge to the forestry track. Follow the path opposite up through the conifers to a stile. Continue ahead up the large field, past a solitary tree and on to a stile in a fence corner – *with a good view of the Clwydian Hills*. Follow the waymarked path along the edge of three fields and down the middle of the next field to go through a gate. Continue down the field to a gate in the corner onto a lane. Follow it LEFT. (For **Walk B** follow the lane down to join your outward route.)

2 After a gate, turn LEFT and follow the signposted Mynydd Hiraethog trail up the stony track to eventually cross a stile by a barn. Go past the old farm and along an enclosed green track to a stile. Continue up to another stile, then go up a green track. After a stile follow a path through the forest to a road. Follow it RIGHT, then take a path on the left signposted to Pincyn Llys. Follow the path through the trees to a forestry track, then continue up the waymarked path to reach the Bagot monument on Pincyn Llys. From the east side of the monument take a path heading south through gorse, soon descending steeply through conifers to a forestry road junction. (For a gentler, if wetter descent, follow the waymarked path west from the monument down to a forestry road. At the nearby junction bear right, now joining the other route to the road.)

3 Turn RIGHT up the first forestry road and follow it past past others for nearly ½ mile to a minor road. Continue along the road for about ¾ mile. At a T- junction turn RIGHT. At crossroads, continue along the lane ahead on a signposted path. Shortly after passing a farm entrance, take a signposted path on the right along a green track to a stile and on across open pasture. After another stile descend to a gate by a ruin, then continue along the enclosed green track. At Cae Gwyn, turn LEFT down its long access lane, then follow the road into Cyffylliog..

WALK 4
PINCYN LLYS FROM CLOCAENOG

DESCRIPTION A 6-mile walk along open side valleys and through forest to Pincyn Llys, on part of the Mynydd Hiraethog trail from and back to Clocaenog. Allow about 3 hours.
START Clocaenog [SJ 084542]
DIRECTIONS Clocaenog is signposted from the B5105 Cerrigydrudion – Ruthin road. Park tidily near the junction opposite the school.

6

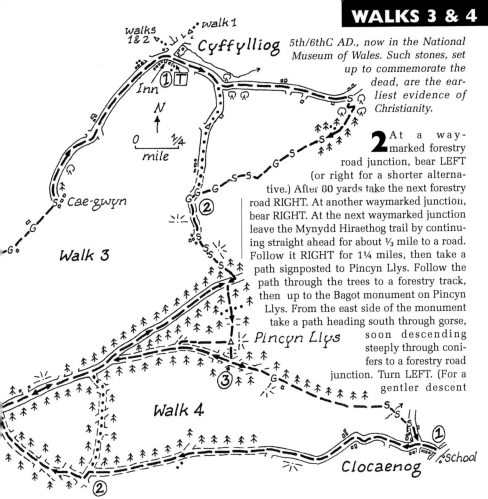

5th/6thC AD., now in the National Museum of Wales. Such stones, set up to commemorate the dead, are the earliest evidence of Christianity.

2 At a way-marked forestry road junction, bear LEFT (or right for a shorter alternative.) After 80 yards take the next forestry road RIGHT. At another waymarked junction, bear RIGHT. At the next waymarked junction leave the Mynydd Hiraethog trail by continuing straight ahead for about ⅓ mile to a road. Follow it RIGHT for 1¼ miles, then take a path signposted to Pincyn Llys. Follow the path through the trees to a forestry track, then up to the Bagot monument on Pincyn Llys. From the east side of the monument take a path heading south through gorse, soon descending steeply through conifers to a forestry road junction. Turn LEFT. (For a gentler descent follow the waymarked Mynydd Hiraethog path west from the monument down to a forestry road junction, then on to point **3**.)

3 Go along the forestry road, descending its right fork to join another across an open area, then take the signposted Mynydd Hiraethog path on the right. Follow the delightful green track – with views of Llantisilio and Berwyn mountains – past a cottage. Continue down the track, then near the valley bottom, cross a stile on the right. Descend half-LEFT to cross a footbridge over a stream, and go on over a stile. Go across the next field and over a stile in the far corner onto a road. Turn RIGHT into Clocaenog.

I Take the road opposite the school and follow it past houses. When it bends right by the former National School – *built by Lord Bagot and once catering for 60 children daily and 45 on Sundays* – go up a lane to St Foddyd's church. *Dating from 1538 and restored in the 19thC, it contains a fine 16thC rood screen, a 15thC font, and a bell, dating from 1638, which is still rung before each service.* Continue along the leafy lane, passing a large old farm. After about ¾ mile, when the lane swings left to a cattle grid, continue up the track ahead. When it meets a forestry road keep ahead. *Near here was found a pillar-stone inscribed in Latin and Ogham script to 'Similinus Tovisacus' – dating from*

WALK 5

CWM ALWEN

DESCRIPTION A 7-mile walk (A) exploring the attractive wooded Alwen valley and its adjoining low hills, lying between the communities of Llanfihangel Glyn Myfyr and Pentre-Llyn Cymmer, featuring pleasant riverside walking, good views and an iron-age fort. Allow about 3½ hours. The route includes a shorter 4½ mile walk (B).

START Llanfihangel Glyn Myfyr [SH 987496]

DIRECTIONS From Cerrigydrudion, take the B5105 towards Ruthin, and after descending the steep hill into Llanfihangel, turn left on a minor road just before the bridge and the Crown Inn. Continue along the road, past the church and shortly you will reach riverside picnic parking areas, just before the former school.

Llanfihangel Glyn Myfyr was the birthplace of Owain Myfyr (Owen Jones) in 1749, a successful London businessman, with an interest in old Welsh manuscripts. His collection formed the basis of the 'Myfyrian Archaiology of Wales' published with his help.

1 Walk back along the road near the river, soon passing St Michael's church – *which was flooded to a height of 9 feet in 1781* – to reach the B5105. Turn LEFT over the splendid single arched stone bridge carrying the road over the Afon Alwen and past the Crown Inn – *an old drovers inn.* Continue up the right hand side of the road and just before the second bend, cross a waymarked stile on the left. Go ahead a few yards, then follow the path up through the trees, passing above a stream. Continue near the stream up the edge of a large field to cross a stile. *Pause to look back at the extensive views your short climb has achieved.* Cross a stony track, then follow the left-hand bank of the stream then go across to a waymark post at the small plantation corner. Follow the waymarked path along the left hand edge of a small lake, passing beneath a small rocky escarpment, then along a long reedy area. After passing a

small pool go on to cross a stile in the fence ahead. Continue across the next two fields passing beneath Foel farm to reach a lane. Turn LEFT along the lane.

2 When the lane passes between two large stone buildings, climb the slope ahead to cross a hidden stile by the roof of the left building. Now go half-LEFT then follow the fence along a long field – *with superb views from the Berwyns in the south to Arenig Fawr in the west* – to go through a gate onto a forestry track. Turn LEFT and follow the track along the forest edge on the eastern edge of Cwm Alwen – *enjoying panoramic views.* After a while the track bends into the forest, later rising to a crossroad of forestry tracks. Here, turn LEFT and follow the track to a road by two houses. Turn LEFT and follow the road down to the river Alwen – *a pleasant place for a break.* (For **Walk B** retrace your steps and about 20 yards from the bridge, turn right by the Clocaenog Forest board into a green track. Follow it along the forest edge parallel with the river below. At the forest end cross a gate, and continue near the river. After crossing a stile, go through the trees to cross the river by a delightful old footbridge to the road. Follow it left back to the start.)

3 Continue up the road, then turn RIGHT along the access lane to Caer Ddunod. Go past the house and continue down the lane to go through a gate just before a white farmhouse, standing beneath the ramparts of Caer Ddunod Iron-Age fort. Go half-LEFT on a waymarked path through two gates between outbuildings and on along an enclosed track. At its end, go through a waymarked gate and walk along the bottom edge of the fort, before crossing a reedy area to a telegraph pole and descending to the river Alwen. Continue beside the river beneath the wooded slopes, over a stile, and along an open stretch of river, soon passing a house opposite. About 150 yards further, after crossing a stream, angle away from the river up and across open pasture to eventually cross a stile just beyond a bend of the river. Continue across the field, over another stile, then go half-LEFT across open pasture, and on along a short track

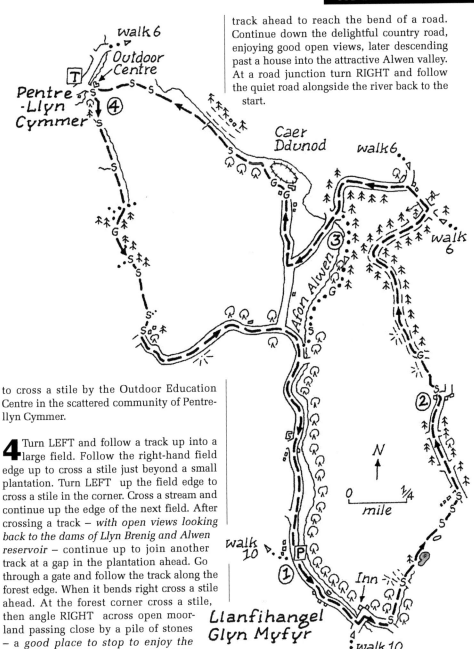

track ahead to reach the bend of a road. Continue down the delightful country road, enjoying good open views, later descending past a house into the attractive Alwen valley. At a road junction turn RIGHT and follow the quiet road alongside the river back to the start.

to cross a stile by the Outdoor Education Centre in the scattered community of Pentre-llyn Cymmer.

4 Turn LEFT and follow a track up into a large field. Follow the right-hand field edge up to cross a stile just beyond a small plantation. Turn LEFT up the field edge to cross a stile in the corner. Cross a stream and continue up the edge of the next field. After crossing a track – *with open views looking back to the dams of Llyn Brenig and Alwen reservoir* – continue up to join another track at a gap in the plantation ahead. Go through a gate and follow the track along the forest edge. When it bends right cross a stile ahead. At the forest corner cross a stile, then angle RIGHT across open moorland passing close by a pile of stones – *a good place to stop to enjoy the extensive views towards the Llantisilio and Berwyn mountains.* Continue on a faint sunken path towards a cottage to cross a stile in the field corner. Follow the green

WALK 6
CRAIG BRON-BANOG

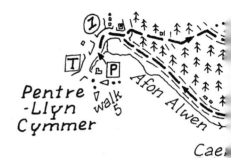

Pentre -Llyn Cymmer

Cae Ddu

DESCRIPTION A 8-mile figure of eight walk (A) exploring the afforested undulating countryside south east of Llyn Brenig, on paths, forestry tracks and quiet lanes. The route meanders through Clocaenog forest, passing a hidden waterfall and ancient standing stone, to its highest point – Craig Bron-Banog at 1610 feet – offering panoramic views. It finishes with a delightful walk along a section of the Alwen river valley, passing by an Iron-Age hillfort. Allow about 4 hours. It can easily be shortened to a 3¼ mile walk (B) or 6 mile walk (C).

START Pentre-Llyn Cymmer [SH 974527]

DIRECTIONS Pentre-Llyn Cymmer, a small scattered farming community, lies east just off the Cerrigydrudion – Llyn Brenig B4501 road. Go through the village, past a chapel and the Outdoor Education Centre. A few hundred yards further is a small roadside parking area on the right opposite a farm.

I Continue along the road, over the river Alwen and on past a house. After the road bends left round past a cottage, take a signposted path on the RIGHT. Follow it up through the trees to reach a forestry track by Cefn y Gors cottage. Cross the track and take the signposted path opposite through conifers, soon crossing an old wall and later descending to a forestry road. Follow it RIGHT, soon skirting upland pasture. As the road begins to bend left, take another track on the right. After ¼ mile the track bends sharp right. Just beyond, take a path on the left descending gently through the trees to cross a delightful small stone bridge over a river. Follow the path up to a forestry track. Turn RIGHT. Down to your right is one of the highlights of the walk – *a beautiful stepped waterfall set amongst the conifers in a deep side valley. If the river is in spate, this makes a wonderful sight.* Now take the LEFT fork of the forestry track up to reach the bend of a road at a prominent viewpoint.

2 Continue ahead along the road, soon descending to Hen Ysgubor and Tal y Cefn Isaf. (For **Walk B** continue with the road, resuming text at point **4**) Here, turn LEFT down a track. At a crossroad of forestry tracks turn RIGHT down the track. It later rises, then runs along the forest edge on the eastern edge of Cwm Alwen – *offering panoramic views* – before bending LEFT to join a road. Go ahead along the road, later passing wall-enclosed upland pasture and old hill farm – *with extensive views south over the forest.* The road then becomes enclosed by forest. (After a few hundred yards, a track on the left angling back into the forest provides a short cut – Walk C – if required.) Continue along the road past a stony track on the left, then a track on the right, after which the road rises more steeply. Shortly after the road levels out – *with views ahead of Llantisilio and Berwyn mountains* – take a signposted path on the left by the old standing stone of Maen Cred – *discovered and re-erected by the Forestry Commission in June 1991* – onto a forestry road. (½ *mile to the east is an Iron-Age village*) When it splits, keep straight ahead up to a crossroad of tracks by a Mynydd Hiraethog trail finger post.

3 Continue up the track ahead, and at another finger post, bend RIGHT with the track up onto the open heather-covered top of Craig Bron- Banog with its transmitter mast. *A notice board advises that the other structures are part of an international project on the effects of climate change in heath-*

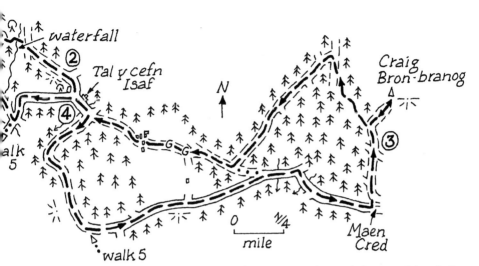

lands. *Do not enter the research area, but enjoy the stunning views: east over Clocaenog Forest to the Clwydian Hills; south east to the Llantisilio Mountains; south west and west to the mountains of Snowdonia; north over Mynydd Hiraethog.* Return down the track to the finger post. Turn RIGHT and follow the signposted path along a green track through the trees to a more defined forestry track. Continue ahead towards distant wind turbines, then at the next forestry track junction, turn LEFT. Keep with the main forestry track, soon descending past a tall transmitter mast and continuing south-west to reach a forestry track T-junction. Turn RIGHT and at a crossroad of forestry tracks, turn LEFT. At the end of the forest go through a gate ahead, and follow a track down to pass through a farm and continue along its access track. At a familiar crossroads of tracks, continue ahead to rejoin the road by Tal y Cefn Isaf. Turn LEFT.

4 Follow the road down and just before a bridge over the river Alwen, take a signposted path along a forestry road on the right. Follow it along the attractive Alwen valley by the edge of the forest, passing the Iron-Age fort of Caer Ddunod visible on the opposite bank of the river, then Ddol uchaf to eventually join your outward route at a road.

Maen Cred

11

WALK 7
LLYN BRENIG

DESCRIPTION A popular 10½ mile way-marked trail around Llyn Brenig, offering ever- changing views of the lake. After crossing the dam of the reservoir, the trail follows a track along its eastern shores, passing Bronze Age burial sites, before taking a path across Gors Maen Llwyd Nature Reserve. It then follows a section of an ancient highway to Pont-y-Brenig, which has many tales to tell, before continuing on a forestry road along the western side of Llyn Brenig. Allow about 4 hours. Other shorter walks by Llyn Brenig include an archaeological trail (see **Walk 8**) and a Nature Trail.

START Llyn Brenig Visitor Centre [SH 968547]

DIRECTIONS Llyn Brenig lies just east of the B4501 Cerrigydrudion-Denbigh road, and is well signposted.

*L*lyn Brenig was first proposed as part of a twin reservoir scheme at the end of the 19thC by the then Corporation of Birkenhead to supply water direct to the town, but only Alwen reservoir was built. When Llyn Brenig was finally constructed between 1973-1976, its purpose was to regulate the flow of the river Dee, providing water for homes and industries in north-east Wales. It is 2½ miles long and 148 feet at its deepest point. It lies over 1200 feet above sea-level, with a climate that is wetter (average rainfall of 52 inches) and 2 – 3 degrees colder than at the coast.

The lake attracts many birds – including great crested grebe, cormorant, and heron, wintering mallard, teal and goldeneye and in spring, willow warblers return. The lake contains brown and locally reared rainbow trout and supports fly fishing, windsurfing, sailing and canoeing.

The Visitor Centre contains a shop, café and an interesting exhibition.

I From the toilets at the end of the Centre descend to the jetty and walk along the lakeside to go through a nearby small gate. Follow the waymarked path above the lake, then across the dam. At its end, continue along a track above the lake. Keep with the main track as it winds its way along the eastern shore of Llyn Brenig, passing through a forest and on by the edge of pastureland/moorland – *with views of a nearby windfarm. Also prominent on the skyline to the north west is the ruin of Gwylfa Hiraethog, the former shooting lodge of the first Viscount Devonport, a politician and first chairman of the Port of London Authority. It was built in 1913 to replace a wooden lodge, made in Norway and erected at 1,627 feet on the moors in the early 1890s. It was an impressive large stone building designed by Sir Edwin Cooper, a notable architect, and had commanding views. It was used as a residence for family and guests, including Lloyd George, during the grouse-shooting season until 1925, when it was sold. The family travelled in a special railway coach from London to Denbigh, before continuing their journey by horse wagon. A notable landmark on the Denbigh moors, it is often referred to as the 'Haunted House', and has featured in several films.* The track loops inland to pass near Hafotty Sion Llwyd – *once a home for shepherds or bailiffs* – then passes a Bronze Age Ring Cairn and burial mound to reach a car park and toilets.

2 Go up the road and after about ⅓ mile, take the waymarked path on the left. The trail meanders across Gors Maen Llwyd Nature Reserve, passing near the old standing stone of Maen Llwyd. *Managed by the North Wales Wildlife Trust since 1988, the Reserve consists of heather moorland and peat bog, rich in plants and insects, which in turn support many small birds – eg. skylark, stonechat, and whinchat. The moorland habitat is particularly important for the increasingly rare Red and Black Grouse.* After a while, the path runs alongside the road before continuing through a clump of trees and rising gently through heather.

3 At a path junction by a waymark post, turn RIGHT back towards the road, then follow a green track, which runs near the road, passing a parking area at Bryn Maen. *This track is the old road from Pentrefoelas to Denbigh, which was replaced in 1826 by* the turnpike road, now the A543. Near Bryn Maen once stood a cottage occupied in the 19thC by a reputed miser with a hoard of golden sovereigns, who had seven locks on his door. Legend tells that after heavy snow, he discovered the remains of his elderly neighbour half eaten by her cat! The track later becomes a path, which then angles away from the road down along-side the forest. After going through a gate, follow a track through the forest to a forestry road/ track crossroads.

4 Continue ahead down the forestry road to reach Pont-y-Brenig by the Nature Trail board. *Pont-y-Brenig, where the old Pentrefoelas-Denbigh road crossed the river, was once described as the most isolated place in North Wales, when the crossing of this wild inhospitable moorland could be a daunting experience for travellers. During the 18thC a local man Foulke Owen passed over this bridge during winter on his return from Denbigh, but never reached home. His body was found some weeks later buried in snow about one mile to the west at the precise spot where his wife dreamt that he had gone to sleep! Heilyn, a local highwayman, reputedly hid under the bridge waiting to rob drovers and farmers on their way back from Denbigh market. Folklore also tells of a young man who met a mysterious stranger dressed in grey clothes with gold buttons here. The stranger smiled, jumped off the bridge and vanished into the bog. Each time the young man passed that way he found a small pile of money and valuables at the same spot!* Continue up the

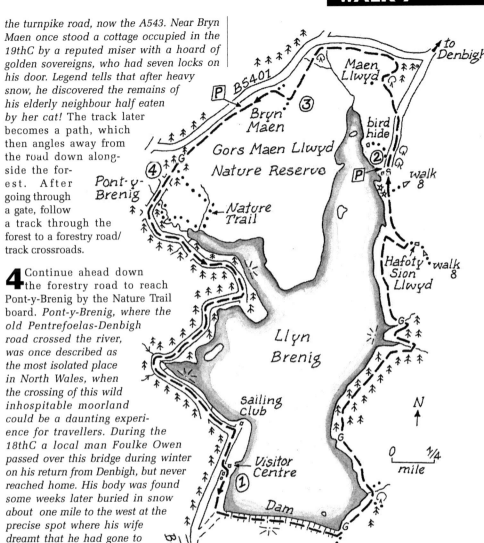

road to another road/track crossroad. Turn LEFT and follow the road as it meanders along the western side of the lake. The road passes cleared sections of forest giving good views of the lake, then the main exit road and the sailing club to eventually reach the Visitor Centre..

WALK 8

ON THE TRAIL OF OUR ANCESTORS

DESCRIPTION This 2½ mile walk follows a waymarked Archaelogical Trail established by the Welsh Water Authority through undulating upland pasture adjoining Llyn Brenig on its north east side. It visits some of the important Bronze Age ceremonial and burial sites, and other places of archaelogical interest investigated between 1973 and 1975 during the construction of Llyn Brenig, and offers extensive views. The trail crosses open reedy, occasionally wet ground, and is best undertaken in good weather. Allow about 2 hours.

START Archaelogical trail car park, Llyn Brenig (NE.) [SH 984574]

DIRECTIONS From Cerrigydrudion take the B4501 north past Llyn Brenig, then take the Nantglyn road. After 1½ miles, follow a lane on the right down to a car park by the lake.

I Cross a stile by a gate near the toilets. Follow the lakeside road to the Ring Cairn (**A**). *It served as a ceremonial monument from about 1680 BC. Later it was used as a cremation burial site. Visit nearby Boncyn Arian (**B**) – a large Bronze Age burial mound covering a central grave used about 2000 BC. Nearby is the site of a Mesolithic camp dating from around 5000 BC. once occupied by Stone Age hunters.* Return to the road and cross a stile by a gate. Head half-LEFT up open pasture and on through a reedy area to reach the Hafotai Settlement (**C**). *Dating from the 16thC, several stone huts, probably thatched with heather and rushes, once occupied both sides of the stream. They served as summer dwellings for the people who brought their animals to graze on the moors.* (For a shorter walk, simply follow the nearby stream down to the start.)

2 The waymarked trail now heads south across reedy terrain just beneath the for-

est – *offering views of Llyn Brenig and the Snowdonia mountains.* It then descends and passes through a gate at the forest corner. Cross a stream, and go up the slope ahead to a waymark post on the skyline, and on up the reedy slope. At another waymark post, bear RIGHT to reach the impressive stone Platform Cairn (**D**) at a prominent viewpoint. *Built around 2000 BC. and occupying an earlier site occupied by Bronze Age man, the cairn contained two separate cremation burials – one the remains of an adult and child placed in an urn beneath a large stone.*

3 From the nearby waymark post, go east towards the hilltop wind turbines for about 40 yards, then bear RIGHT to reach an information board overlooking the site of Hen Ddinbych (**E**) – *a large medieval farmhouse.* Descend the slope beneath the board to cross the site and continue to a fence corner. Keep ahead alongside the fence, then cross a stile in the corner. Continue past a waymark post to skirt the bottom of an area of bracken. After about 300 yards, bear RIGHT across the heather covered flat side valley, over a

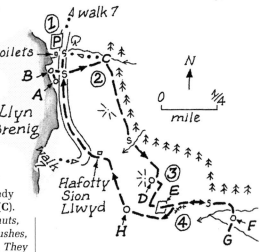

stream, and on to reach a Bronze Age kerb-cairn (**F**) by a white marker post. *The wooden posts mark the post-holes of a possible prehistoric hut, over which the cairn containing a cremation burial was built. Nearby is Maen*

Cleddau **(G)** – *a large glacial stone, reputed to have been broken by a giant's sword.* Retrace your steps to the fence corner at Hen Ddinbych.

4 Now skirt round the southern end of Hen Ddinbych and follow the waymarked trail up the slope to another Bronze Age kerb-cairn **(H)**. Continue towards the northern end of the lake, soon descending a track leading to Hafotty Sion Llwyd. *Rebuilt in 1881 using some stone from Hen Ddinbych, this was the home of shepherds or bailiffs.* Pass in front of the house, then follow the lakeside road back to the start.

Continue ahead, then at a track junction, bear LEFT, soon overlooking a narrow section of the lake (seat). The track then bends away from the lake, later passing an area of cleared forest. The waymarked trail then follows a stony path down through the

trees, soon leaving the forest to rejoin the lake. The path follows the lake edge, then bends inland to cross a stream, and continues through an area of forest, leaving it by a kissing gate. Just beyond, follow the waymarked trail LEFT to join a stony track which descends to a footbridge over the reservoir.

2 After a kissing gate on the other side, the path continues to old sheepfolds, crosses a stream, then rises steadily across open moorland. Shortly after a kissing gate, you reach the highest point of the trail, offering panoramic views. The path now steadily descends to gates/stile and goes down to a forestry track above a stream. The stony trail path continues through young trees, then follows a forestry track. Later the trail angles off the track down towards the lake, bends into a side valley and rises through trees to join another forestry track. When it bends away from the lake, the trail descends towards the lake and continues near the lakeside to cross the dam.

WALK 9
ALWEN TRAIL

DESCRIPTION A 7-mile circuit of Alwen Reservoir, built in the early 20thC to supply water to Birkenhead. The route follows a waymarked trail for walkers and mountain bikers which opened in 2006. It features sections of forest, lakeside and open exposed moorland, reaching a height of 1410 feet/430 metres, and is best undertaken in good conditions. Allow about 4 hours.

START Car park, the dam, Alwen Reservoir. [SH 956530]

DIRECTIONS The Alwen Reservoir is signposted off the B4501, midway on a hill. Follow the stony track, soon taking its left fork. After passing between houses, turn left to park by the impressive dam, whose first stone was laid in October 1911.

1 Go past the dam and on the bend, take the signposted path to Pen-y-Ffrith. The stony trail path, waymarked by blue posts, soon passes through trees to join a forestry track, which you follow past a stone house. Shortly, the track rises and splits into three.

WALK 10
CAER CARADOG

DESCRIPTION A 5½ mile walk (A) through a little visited area of open countryside and upland pasture, with excellent views. The route explores the attractive open undulating countryside west of Cwm Alwen, visiting a small reservoir. Later it rises across open slopes on an old green track to pass Caer Caradog, an Iron-Age hillfort. It continues on a delightful old drovers' road, which contours around the mid-slopes of Mwdwleithin, before descending to Llanfihangel. Allow about 3 hours. A shorter 2½ mile walk (B) is included. .
START Llanfihangel Glyn Myfyr [SH 987496] See **Walk 5**.

I Walk along the road, then just before the.former school take a signposted path through a gate on the left opposite a children's play area. Follow a rising green track above a stream. After a gate the track splits. Take the track bearing RIGHT to go through a gate over the stream, then angle LEFT up the field to rejoin the track. Follow it above the side valley, through a gate, and on through an abandoned farm. Continue up the track, soon crossing the stream, then bending RIGHT into a field. Go up the field and through a gap in its top right hand corner. Follow the track for 15 yards to go through a gap on the left in the gorse-covered boundary. Go up the field and through a gate in its top corner. Go through a gap in the old wall just ahead, and follow the fence/wall on your left up to go through a gate in it, near the corner. (For **Walk B**, follow a gated green track heading south, then a lane, to the B5105. Follow it left. After a few hundred yards go through a gate on the right onto a green track. Follow the track, then lane to a road. Follow it left down into Llanfinghafel).

2 For the main walk go through the gate just above. Turn LEFT (west) across upland pasture – *enjoying extensive views* – soon heading towards ruined buildings by a rocky escarpment. Go past the barn to go through a gate on the right just beyond

a ruined cottage. Go half-LEFT to see the hidden small attractive rowan tree edged reservoir – *home for wildfowl and a quiet spot for fishing*. Retrace your steps, and after passing through the gate by the cottage, go half-RIGHT and through another gate. Walk towards another old cottage, and after about 80 yards, bear LEFT to go through a gate. Turn RIGHT along a green track, past the old smallholding, down to a gate by a finger post. Turn LEFT along a lane, past Maes Tyddyn farm, and on to reach the B5105. Turn RIGHT and walk down the grass verge.

3 After a few hundred yards, take a signposted path through a small gate on the left to pass between a house and an outbuilding. Keep ahead, over a stream, and through a gate. Continue up an enclosed old green track. After another gate, the track rises steadily across the open western slopes of Y Drum – *offering excellent views west towards Cerrigydrudion and the mountains of Snowdonia beyond*. After passing a short section of collapsed wall, the track passes through a gateway, rises near the fence on your right, then soon fades. Keep on with the fence to go through a gate at its highest point. Continue beside the fence, with the distinctive ramparts of Caer Caradog hillfort to your right. *The Iron-Age fort, situated at 1250 feet on a strategic site overlooking important valley routes, has a circular rampart of earth and shale enclosing an area of about 2 acres. It is reputed to be the legendary fortified base of King Caractacus, who was captured by the Romans and taken in chains to Rome.* The fence descends to a gate. Keep ahead, past the fence corner, then go down the middle of the field to cross a ladder-stile onto a minor road. Follow it LEFT and at a junction, keep ahead to pass two farms. When the road bends left, go straight ahead on a green track to a gate, and continue along this delightful enclosed old drovers' road to go through a gate into open country, where you join the Mynydd Hiraethog trail.

4 Continue with the green track near the wall on your left, rising steadily up the hillside. The track passes through two gates, then crosses the grassy slopes of Mwdwl-

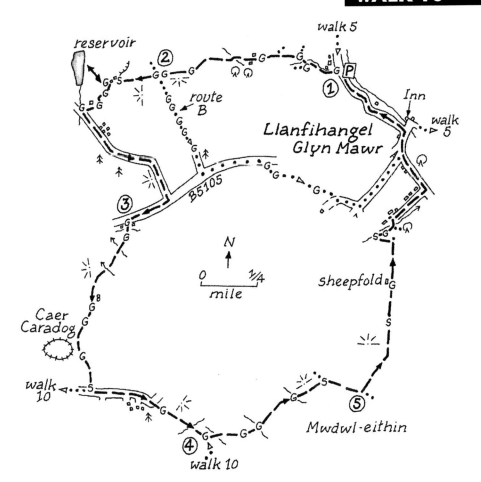

eithin. After another gate, the track continues along the edge of upland pasture and the now heather and bracken covered slopes of Mwdwl-eithin (an open access area). *100 yards from the gate, a section of wall makes an ideal place to stop to take in the views.* When an arm of the track bends down left, cross a stile ahead, and continue along the green track.

5 Just before the next gate on the track, at a waymark post, bend LEFT along another green track on the start of a long gradual descent towards Llanfihangel. After a ladder-stile, keep ahead, then go through a gate by a sheepfold. Now follow an old gorse lined green track down the hillside, and at its end go through a gateway. Turn LEFT down the field edge to cross a stile in the bottom fence corner. Turn RIGHT, go through a gate, and on alongside a stream. Soon cross the stream beneath a red barn, go past a farm and along its access lane. At a junction, turn LEFT along the road into Llanfihangel. At the next junction, turn RIGHT to reach the B5105. Cross the road and follow it to the junction. If not tempted by the nearby Crown Inn – a traditional pub with a scenic beer garden above the river – turn LEFT along the minor road, soon passing St. Michael's church, back to the start.

WALK 11
AROUND CWM CEIRW

DESCRIPTION A 8½ mile walk exploring the remote hills and valleys lying between the ancient communities of Llangwm and Cerrigydrudion, incorporating sections of the Mynydd Hiraethog trail at both ends, offering extensive views. The route rises from Llangwm to high upland pasture above the Ceirw valley (1148 feet/350 metres), then follows an old drovers' route past an Iron-Age hillfort down to Cerrigydrudion. It then rises through open country to pass prominent hillside wind turbines at 1378 feet/420 metres, before descending into side valleys back to Llangwm. Allow about 5 hours.
START Llangwm [SH 966446] or alternative Cerrigydrudion [SH 954488].
DIRECTIONS Llangwm is signposted from the A5. Park tidily by the former village church. See **Walk 12** for the alternative start. Walk through the village to join the route at the A5 (point **4**).

Llangwm is reputed to be the site of a battle in the 10thC when the Prince of South Wales was slain by the Prince of North Wales. Traditionally an agricultural community, where cattle/sheep were fattened before drovers moved them to London markets it was once noted for its large black cattle fair held on 18th April. It also once produced knitted stockings which were sold in London and Liverpool markets.

I Walk north through the village. After crossing the river, continue along the road and about 150 yards after the bend, take a signposted path on the left. Go up through the wood to a small gate, then, go half-LEFT up the field, over a track, and on to cross a stile in the corner. Descend to another stile by a farm, then turn LEFT through a gate at the end of a barn. Cross the farmyard and turn RIGHT through another gate and follow the farm's access track down past a chapel, to a road. Go through the gate opposite and two kissing gates, then walk alongside the river Ceirw. Cross a footbridge over the river and follow an enclosed path to the A5. Turn LEFT, then cross the road and follow the signposted path through the farm opposite. Go through a gate at the right-hand side of the house, then follow a track behind outbuildings. The track now meanders steadily up the hillside. At its end continue up the field edge. After about 150 yards, turn LEFT over a stile, and go along the field edge and through a gate by a large barn.

2 Continue up the stony track (arrow misleading) passing to the right of the large farm, then bear RIGHT along another track – with new views towards Snowdonia. The track rises to a second stile and continues by the fence, soon bending up to two gates. Go through the higher one. Continue ahead by the wall on your left to go through a gate in the field corner. Keep beside the wall. After crossing a stile, bear LEFT with the wall down to a finger post. Here you leave the Mynydd Hiraethog trail by turning LEFT through a gate and following a delightful enclosed old drovers' track up to a road. Go along the road ahead past farms.

3 At a junction keep ahead, soon passing Caer Caradog Iron-Age fort up to your right. (See **Walk 7**). Continue with this quiet upland road – *an old drovers' route offering extensive views* – soon steadily descending towards distant Cerrigydrudion. At a white cottage in the dip turn LEFT along a track leading to Fron Deg. Follow it past the house, bending up through a small caravan site to a kissing gate. Continue along the edge of two fields, past a barn, and down a track to the road in Cerrigydrudion. Follow the short path opposite to the A5. Cross the road with care and follow the pavement past a cafe and The Saracens Head. *Note the old milestone. Holyhead, Corwen – but where is Cernioge? See Walk 14 for the answer.*

4 Turn LEFT along a minor road and follow it over the river, past houses and up to a junction. Turn LEFT past Pen-y-Bryn Bach. Shortly, the road heads into open country towards distant wind turbines. Just after passing a farm on your right, take a signposted path through a gate. Go across the field to cross a stile. Go along the next field edge to a ruined cottage. Turn LEFT down to a gate, and on to cross a footbridge over the Afon Ceirw. Continue near the

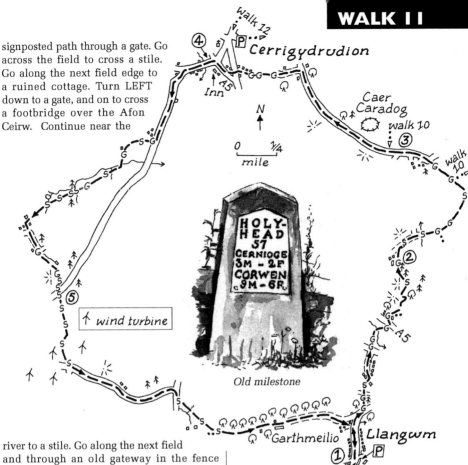

Old milestone

river to a stile. Go along the next field and through an old gateway in the fence ahead. Continue to pass through a narrow strip of woodland (stiles), then follow the stiled path across two fields to enter a large field with small pool nearby. Now bear LEFT towards the left-hand side of a large farm. Pass between outbuildings, then bend LEFT up to join and follow the farm's access lane. At a bend by a stone building go through the middle of three gates. Go up the right bank of the stream and on to reach an old boundary embankment/fence. Here, turn RIGHT alongside the boundary, soon going through a gate in it. Continue with the boundary to cross a stile and another ahead onto the road.

5 Cross the stile opposite to join the Mynydd Hiraethog trail back to Llangwm. Follow the stiled path up two fields towards the wind turbines, then go

ahead past a reedy area, then bear RIGHT to pass beneath the higher rock escarpment to cross a stile. Follow the fence on the left past one turbine to a stile onto a road. Follow it LEFT down to the B4501 then turn RIGHT. After 100 yards, take the signposted path over a stile on the left. Keep ahead down the field edge, cross a stream and follow the fence to cross a stile in the corner. Keep ahead, then after about 150 yards, angle down the slope to cross a stile in the corner onto a track. Follow the track beneath a wood, passing Gamekeepers Cottage, then Garthmeilio – *an impressive 14thC estate house.* Continue along its driveway. Later, as it bends towards the road, keep ahead on a green track past cottages to reach the road.

WALK 12
CRAIG YR IYRCHEN

DESCRIPTION A 6½ mile walk (**A**) exploring attractive upland pasture and moorland fringes north of Cerrigydrudion, rising in stages to a height of over 1400 feet with excellent views. The route crosses lower pastures, then rises very steadily up a quiet lane, before following a waymarked path across the upper slopes of Craig yr Iyrchen. It then descends to the ancient hamlet of Cefn Brith, before returning by road and field paths. Allow about 3½ hours. The route also offers a simple 1¼ walk (**B**).

START Cerrigydrudion [SH 954488]

DIRECTIONS Cerrigydrudion lies just off the A5. There is a signposted car park alongside a garage at the beginning of Ruthin Road (B5105)

Cerrigydrudion is the largest settlement in Mynydd Hiraethog. Its name meaning 'the stones of the daring ones' is reputedly a reference to a large pile of stones once located near the church. Local tradition says that they were the prison in which Cyn-vrig Rwth, a lawless chieftain, kept his captives. The original 18thC London–Holyhead turnpike coach road once passed through the village centre, but in the early 19thC, Thomas Telford diverted the route, building a new road from Cerrigydrudion to Glasfryn, now the A5. Much of the surrounding grazing land was let to Anglesey dealers for fattening up their cattle on the way to the Midland markets. The village was an important shoeing station and one of its famous sons was the 17thC drover and poet, Edward Morus – still droving at 82! In the 19thC villagers were involved in cattle/sheep breeding, spinning of woollen yarn and knitting of stockings. There used to be five fairs a year. In 1854, George Borrow, the eminent traveller and writer of 'Wild Wales' stayed at 'the Lion – whether the white, black, red or green Lion I do not know' after walking 20 miles from Llangollen on his way to Bangor. Here he enjoyed good conversation with a doctor and a Welsh-speaking Italian. In the centre stands St. Mary Magdalene's church, dating from the 16thC and restored in 1874, and almshouses built in 1716.

I Walk along Ruthin Road to reach the driveway to Bwlch-y-beudy at the outskirts of Cerrigydrudion. *On the skyline beyond the white cottage ahead are the distinctive ramparts of Caer Caradog Iron-Age hillfort.* Turn up the driveway, then take a signposted path over a ladder-stile on the left. Follow the stiled path along the edge of four fields – *enjoying good views over Cerrigydrudion, and towards the mountains of Snowdonia* – to reach the B4501. Go along the road opposite towards Cefn Brith, soon passing a house, then a stile on the left about 100 yards beyond (the short/return route). Continue along the road. After passing a stream and a driveway on the right the road rises gently.

2 At a junction, turn RIGHT and go up the minor road. After a while it levels out to provide panoramic views west along the wide valley towards the mountains of Snowdonia. This delightful walled road continues up the hillside, past a side road and a house. At the next junction keep ahead to pass beneath Parc Newydd. After a gate the more open lane rises gently across upland pasture grazed by sheep – *soon with views east to wind turbines above Clocaenog Forest, and ahead to the forest hiding Alwen reservoir, later glimpsing the dam tower among the trees.*

3 Eventually you reach Craig-yr-iyrchen-fawr. Here take the signposted path over a stile on the left and go up the stony track. *Visible on the skyline to the north, is the ruin of Gwylfa Hiraethog – the former shooting lodge of Viscount Devonport (for details see* **Walk 7***).* After about 250 yards, at the first of two small quarries, take the waymarked path angling up the slope on the left, past another waymark post and on to cross a stile in a fence. *Looking back you can now see Alwen reservoir.* Now angle away from the fence up the tussocky ground, over a small rise and on to a waymark post at a prominent viewpoint on Craig yr Lyrchen. (Or follow the waymarked path up alongside the fence for about 100 yards to a waymarked fence post, then bear RIGHT across the tussocky/heather terrain to the waymark post.) *Enjoy the views east to Clocaenog Forest; south east to the Llantisilio Mountains; south to the Berwyns; and south west to the Aran and Arenig mountains.* Continue ahead on a green track. *New views unfold westwards to Llyn y Cwrt and the mountains of Snowdonia.* The track gently descends to a waymark post, then angles down the upland pasture. At another waymark post follow the waymarked path through the edge of an area of heather, past another post in open ground, and on through more heather to cross a ladder-stile – *a good place for a break to enjoy the extensive views. Snowdon, Moel Siabod, the Glyders, Tryfan and the Carneddau range dominate the skyline on a clear day.*

4 Turn LEFT along the track, soon steadily descending the hillside. After a gate continue down a walled lane. At a crossroad, in the hamlet of Cefn Brith, turn LEFT, and at the next junction, continue ahead. Follow the quiet country road back towards Cerrigydrudion for about 1½ miles, later joining your outward route. *This was the original 18thC turnpike road.* Just before the house on the left, cross the stile on the right. Walk alongside the wall and cross another stile in the corner. Turn LEFT alongside the wall

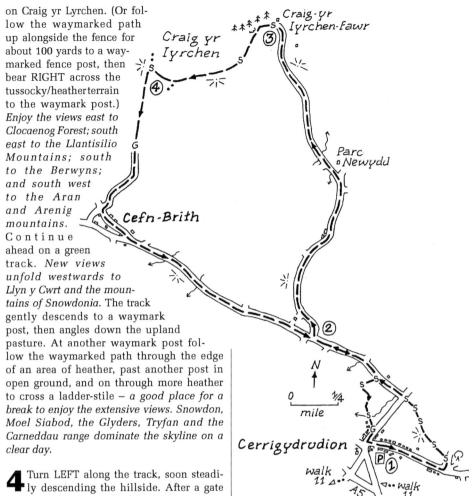

down to go through a gateway in the corner. Turn RIGHT and follow the wall down the field for about 120 yards, then go half-LEFT to cross a stile by a stream. Go across a reedy area and up the field edge to reach the road opposite the school. Turn RIGHT to reach the centre of Cerrigydrudion.

WALK 13
CWM PENANNER

DESCRIPTION This 6½ mile walk explores a little-known area of upland pasture and the hidden attractive valley of Cwm Penanner with its scattered farming community. The route, which uses quiet country roads, field paths and a superb open upland bridleway, offers a great sense of space and excellent ever changing distant views. It can easily be shortened or varied, with additional link paths/road shown. Allow about 3½ hours.

START Crossroads above Cwm Penanner [SH 918480]

DIRECTIONS From Glasfryn, take the minor road heading south off the A5, opposite a pottery. Follow it past a side road to rise steadily up the hillside to reach the signposted Bala, Cerrigydrudion, Blaen Cwm, Glasfryn crossroads, where there is off-road parking.

I Walk back along the road towards Glasfryn, and after nearly ⅓ mile, take a signposted path through a gate on the right. Keep ahead to pass to the left of a ruined cottage (The Lodge), over a stream and on to cross a stile. Now follow a stiled path along the edge of several fields – *said to have been regularly walked by an elderly lady, the last occupant of the cottage, on her way to church in Cerrigydrudion* – to a road. Continue ahead along the road. Shortly take a signposted path through a gate on the right opposite a small ruin. Ignore the track leading to a transmitter mast, but go half-RIGHT up the field – *with a good view across to Snowdon, the Glyders and Carneddau mountains* – and on to the wall/fence corner by two telegraph poles – *offering your first view into the hidden Cwm Penanner, with wind-turbines on the high ridge, and the Llangwm hills beyond.* Go past the gateway and continue alongside the fence on your left. When it joins a wall just ahead, angle gently away from the boundary to cross a stile by a sheepfold and gate in the field corner. Go round the left hand edge of a reedy area and on through a gate onto a nearby farm's access lane.

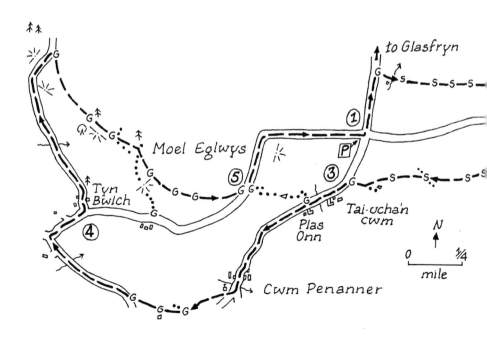

2 Cross the stile opposite, then go half-LEFT to join the fence on your left above the farm. At its corner, continue ahead across the slope, passing just below rock outcrops, then descending to cross a stile in the boundary corner. Follow the wall on your right to cross a stile at its end in a corner. Continue near the boundary on your left to go through a gap in the field corner, and cross a fence just ahead. Keep ahead past gorse to cross a track and a stile in the fence just beyond. Now bear half-RIGHT across the large field, soon descending to cross a stile the fence ahead about 120 yards above a ruin. Angle down across rough pasture to join a track, which you follow to a road. Turn LEFT.

3 Follow the road past Tai-ucha'n-cwm – *note the Lion 1720 datestone on the front of the house* – and on past Plas Onn. (For **Walk B**, go through a gate opposite the gable end of the house and follow a green track that winds its way up the hillside to a higher road at point **5**.) Follow the road to steadily descend into Cwm Penanner to reach the chapel by the river and a road junction. *The chapel built in 1898 continues to serve this scattered community.* A signpost indicates that you are only 7 miles from Bala! Continue past the chapel, through a gate and at the corner of the churchyard, leave the road on the signposted path, which follows the boundary on your right across reedy terrain. Later the clear path angles away from the boundary to go through a waymarked gate. Follow the boundary on your right, and at its first corner

after about 25 yards, take a stone-paved path part hidden in the reeds to your left. Follow this intermittent paved path through another reedy area to go through a gate by a cottage. Continue ahead with the path along the left-hand edge of a large reedy area, by an old field boundary. When it bends right, keep ahead across the field to go through a small wooden gate in the boundary ahead to rejoin the road. Follow it up to a junction. Turn RIGHT and follow the road up to another junction.

4 Turn LEFT up past Tyn Bwlch. Follow the road for about ¾ mile beneath the eastern slopes of Garn Prys. After a level section the road bends down towards the expansive valley – *with the mountains of Snowdonia visible to the north-west.* As the road becomes less steep, you reach two gates on the right. Here go through the higher gate and up a green track (a bridleway). It soon levels out and continues across upland pasture, passing through a gate, then between an area of young trees and a small plantation – *with excellent open views.* After another gate, keep ahead. When the track splits, continue ahead on the higher fork, soon crossing a cross-track and rising to a gate. This delightful scenic gated green track continues round the higher slopes of Moel Eglwys – *offering panoramic views as far as the Berwyns and Arans* – before descending gently to the road.

5 Turn LEFT and follow this delightful high-level road contouring the eastern slopes of Moel Eglwys and upland pasture back to the start.

Chapel in Cwm Penanner

LLYN Y CWRT

DESCRIPTION A 6½ mile meandering walk (A) across the lower northern slopes of the wide Cwm Merddwr valley near Glasfryn, featuring a small attractive hidden upland lake, an old coaching inn, now a farm, delightful old walled tracks and extensive views. The route follows a section of the Mynydd Hiraethog trail across upland pasture, reaching a height of just over 1100 feet, before descending to Cernioge. It then heads north past Llyn y Cwrt to join the outward route, before making a direct return. Allow about 3½ hours. The route offers two shorter walks of 2 miles (**B**) and 4½ miles (**C**).

START Glasfryn [SH 917502]

DIRECTIONS Glasfryn lies on the A5 mid-way between Pentrefoelas and Cerrigydrudion. Car parking in the village is time restricted, so park in a lay-by at the western end of the village

I Walk east along the A5 through the village, then take the side road signposted to Cefn Brith by the old school. After nearly ½ mile on a bend, cross a waymarked stile on the left to join the Mynydd Hiraethog trail. Angle up the field to join a wall on the left. Follow the wall to cross a footbridge, then on to cross a stone stile in the field corner. Continue along the next field edge to cross a ladder-stile. Go through the gate ahead, and keep ahead along an old walled green track – *enjoying extensive views from the Berwyns to the mountains of Snowdonia. Also visible is Llyn y Cwrt.* After going through a gate, continue ahead, now with the wall on your right, to reach a crossroad of walled tracks. (For **Walk B** turn left.)

2 Follow the enclosed track ahead, soon descending to cross a river, and on up to go through a gate ahead by another track. Go through a gate ahead, and walk alongside the wall on your left, over a stream and a stile, and up the edge of the next field. After crossing a stile continue ahead along a small grassy ridge past a waymark post. *On a clear day, Moel Siabod, Snowdon, the Glyders,*

Tryfan and the Carneddau range dominate the skyline ahead. To your right is the high moorland ridge of Mwdwl-eithin. At a finger post, where a green track angles in from the left (your return route), keep ahead on the waymarked trail. Go on through a wall gap and over a stile. Follow the wall to reach another finger post.

3 Here you leave the trail by turning LEFT through a gate. Follow a walled track down to an an old hillfarm. Pass between the house and outbuilding, then bear LEFT to go through a gate below a corrugated barn. Go across the field and through a gate in the corner. Go across the next large field to cross a stone stile by a gate in the top corner. Now follow the boundary on the left round and down the long field – *with a good view of Llyn y Cwrt fringed by alder woodland* – to a gate in the bottom corner. Keep ahead alongside the fence, through a gate, and on along a track to join the farm's access drive. Follow it down to the A5, to see Cernioge Mawr opposite. (For **Walk C** simply walk along the pavement on the A5 for ½ mile back to the start.)

4 Return along the track for 60 yards, then bear RIGHT to go through a gate in the wall corner. Turn LEFT up the field edge, through a gate in the corner, and continue ahead to go through a gate at the wood corner. Go along the wood edge to reach Llyn y Cwrt with its stone boathouse. Continue along the lake edge, through a gate and on through another gate just beyond the lake corner. Go across the field, through a gate, then across the next field above the lake to another gate. Continue across a further field to the far boundary and follow it up to the farm to go through a gate in the corner by the house. Bear LEFT along a track between farm buildings, then go through a gate up on the right. Follow a gated track up a shallow side valley to reach the finger post passed earlier. Now follow your outward route back to the crossroad of walled tracks at point **2**. Turn RIGHT and follow the enclosed track down to a house. Go through a gate on the right at the end of the house, then follow its access track to the A5 by the garage. Turn LEFT back to the start.

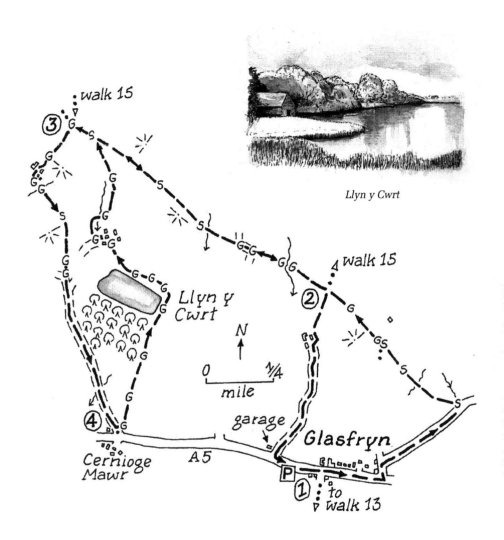

Llyn y Cwrt

About the author, David Berry

David is an experienced walker with a love of the countryside and an interest in local history. He is the author of a series of walks guidebooks covering North Wales, where he has lived and worked for many years, as well as a freelance writer for Walking Wales magazine. He has worked as a Rights of Way surveyor across North Wales and is a member of Denbighshire Local Access Forum. He hopes that his comprehensive guides will encourage people to explore on foot its diverse scenery and rich heritage.

WALK 15

MWDWL-EITHIN

DESCRIPTION An exhilarating 8¼ mile walk around the remote high moorland ridge of Mwdwl-eithin, now an Open Access area, lying between the A5 and the A543, offering excellent views. The route rises to cross the broad ridge at 1500 feet, skirts its eastern slopes, then joins the Alwen trail to descend to a side valley near the neck of the Alwen reservoir. It then follows an ancient green road up to a bwlch, before descending across moorland and returning via field paths and tracks. This moorland romp, wet in places, is for experienced, well equipped walkers only and should be avoided in poor visibility. Allow about 5 hours.
START Glasfryn [SH 917502] See **Walk 14**.

1 Follow the instructions contained in the first section of Walk 14.

2 Here, turn RIGHT over old gates and follow the walled track up the hillside – *used by drovers to move cattle and sheep from upland pastures on their journey to distant markets.* Go through a gateway and continue up the track. At its end by sheepfolds, cross a stile into open upland country. Continue along the near-side edge of a small grassy ridge, passing to the left of a reedy area. After about 200 yards, bear LEFT on a green track. Take its LEFT fork, faint at first, but soon more distinct, to ford a stream. Now bear RIGHT to follow a clear path parallel with an old wall on your left. After crossing a stream, keep ahead on a faint green track, with the remains of the wall on your left, to go through a gate in a more substantial wall ahead.

3 Continue ahead to follow a clear path rising steadily up the heather covered southern slopes of Mwdwl-eithin towards two small trees on the horizon. Later, the path becomes more intermittent as it passes through bracken. Keep ahead to pass to the right of the small hill on which stand the two trees, then follow a path up a tussocky/reedy area, passing another two small trees to your

right. Keep ahead along the edge of heather-covered high ground to your left, passing just to the right of another small tree. The path continues up through heather, then levels out – *with views across to the summit cairns on Mwdwl-eithin and beyond the mountains of Snowdonia.*

4 The path now skirts beneath the heather-covered high ground to your right, then crosses a more expansive area of heather – *with views now across to Alwen reservoir and its surrounding forest. Prominent on the distant skyline to the NE. is the ruined shooting lodge of Gwylfa Hiraethog (see* **Walk 7***).* Follow the clear path heading north as it first contours, then steadily descends across the bracken and heather covered eastern slopes of Mwdwl-eithin. It then crosses a level wet reedy area. After passing above a small ruin continue in the same direction across drier moorland to eventually join the stony Alwen trail at its highest point, with a kissing gate below. (An alternative path on the ground takes you towards a visible gate at the end of cleared forest, where you can join the trail earlier and follow it up the hillside.)

5 From the kissing gate follow the trail down into a side valley. Immediately after crossing a stream, turn LEFT and go past sheepfolds to reach a tree by the small ruin of Nant Heilyn – *the former home of Heilyn, an 18thC highwayman, who used to rob drovers and farmers on their way home from Denbigh market. His hoard of stolen silver and gold may still lie hidden nearby!* It makes a good stopping place. Now follow an old green track up the hillside, later passing through a gate. *This is the remains of the old Denbigh – Pentrefoelas road, which was replaced by a turnpike road, now the A543, in 1826.* Eventually, when you reach level ground – *with views towards Llyn Alwen and the mountains of Snowdonia beyond* – follow the line of the old track as it contours SW. across tussocky/reedy ground, with the A543 below. Later keep to its left bank to eventually go through a gate visible on the skyline ahead – *with a view of Llyn Alwen, Llyn Aled and Aled Isaf.* Continue ahead to follow a path across the moorland, where

and bracken terrain, between the stream and higher ground to your left. After a while, as the line of the stream begins to make a noticeable descent into a valley, and when in line with a large pile of boulders beyond the stream, the path angles away from the stream towards a distant fence. Go through the higher of two gates at a fence junction. Follow the boundary on your right across open pasture and through another gate. Keep ahead alongside the boundary, and its corner, continue ahead to rejoin the Mynydd Hiraethog trail by a finger post.

7 Continue with the wall on your right to cross a stile and go through a wall gap. Pass another finger post and waymark post to walk along a grassy ridge, past another post, and on to cross a stile. Keep ahead down the field edge to cross a stile in the corner. Keep ahead, over a stream, and on alongside the wall to go through a gate in the field corner – *with a good view of Llyn y Cwrt. Go along a track and through a gate ahead, then follow a track down, over a river and on up to reach the crossroad of walled tracks met at point 2. Turn RIGHT and follow the enclosed track down to a house. Go through a gate on the right at the end of the house, then follow its access track to the A5 by the garage. Turn LEFT back to the start.*

little remains of the old road, to reach the top of the high pass of Bwlch y Garnedd at a prominent new viewpoint. Descend the wide embanked old green road.

6 After a few hundred yards, at a large boulder to the left, head half-LEFT down tussocky terrain to go through a gate in the fence below. Cross an adjoining stile and the stream ahead, then bear RIGHT to follow an intermittent path across reed, heather

WALK 16
CWM MERDDWR

DESCRIPTION A 5¾ mile walk (**A**) exploring the undulating countryside of the Merddwr valley near Pentrefoelas. The route features a delightful old drovers' road, a historical house, a 12thC motte and excellent views. Allow about 3 hours. A shorter 3¾ mile walk (**B**) is included.

START Car park, Pentrefoelas [SH 874 514]

DIRECTIONS In Pentrefoelas leave the A5 and take the road opposite the Foelas Arms Hotel across the river past the Riverside Chocolate House to a car park and nearby toilets.

Pentrefoelas is an attractive estate village built by the Wynne family for its workers and craftsmen. Its water-powered mill, which still remains, was used to ground grain for bread or animal fodder. It was once an important gathering place for cattle and drovers, and in the 19thC a stopping place on Telford's London-Holyhead coach road. The three-storey Foelas Arms Hotel was enlarged in 1839 when it took on the licence from a well known coaching house situated at Cernioge, some 2½ miles to the east. The village now boasts an hotel, craft shop, gallery, and a post office/general stores/café.

It is associated with fairies and folklore. One tale involves Huw Llwyd, a famous Welsh sorcerer, who lived in Snowdonia. While staying at Pentrefoelas, he was approached by four thieves who thought he was a drover returning from the English market with money. He caused them to be transfixed overnight by a magic horn, which vanished when they were arrested the following morning!

I Go back towards the A5, then take the signposted path through a small gate on the left just before the bridge. Walk along the field edge near the river. After about 200 yards, the waymarked path angles away from the river and rises to pass through a gateway. Now go half-LEFT up the next field to a stile by trees and go through a small gate above. Angle up the field to cross the ladder-stile ahead – *with views of the mountains of Snowdonia.* Turn LEFT and follow the waymarked path round the field edge to go through a gate by stone enclosures. Turn LEFT and descend the track to go through a gate in the field corner at a signposted path junction.

2 Turn LEFT through an adjoining gate and follow the green track – *part of the original late 18thC London-Holyhead coach road* – to a road junction. Here do a U-turn along the nearby road. After about 250 yards, cross a waymarked ladder-stile on the left. Follow a faint green track up the field to a stile in the top corner. Keep ahead past a barn and a caravan, and follow a green track up to a stile by a gate. Continue up the track, then just before it enters a gateway, turn LEFT along the field edge to a gate in the corner. Continue ahead along the edge of the next field to a ladder-stile by Plas Iolyn. Go ahead, and at the end of the barn, bear LEFT to pass between outbuildings then the house, and follow its driveway to a lane. *Plas Iolyn, with its 18thC wing, is dominated by the stone 'Great Barn' built high up on a rock. The house was once occupied by the notorious Dr. Ellis Price, a Doctor of Law, whose red robe earned him the name of 'Dr. Coch' (Red Doctor) His son, Capt. Thomas Price – a seafaring man and poet, along with Capt. Will Myddelton of Denbigh, are said to have been the first men to 'drink' (smoke) tobacco in public in this country.*

3 Turn sharp RIGHT along the lane. Shortly, you will catch sight of the 17thC Giler gatehouse. *Giler itself, dating from the 16thC, was once the home of poet Rhys Wynn and the Price family descended from Cardinal Wolsey's cross-bearer.* On the bend, continue through the waymarked gate ahead. Now follow a delightful old enclosed gated green drovers' road for about ¾ mile, skirting the small hill of Bryn Prys. After a third gate, the route begins to descend – *with extensive mountain views* – becoming a more defined stony track. (For **Walk B**, cross a stile on the right and follow the waymarked Mynydd Hiraethog path along an enclosed green track down to pass through a farm and along its

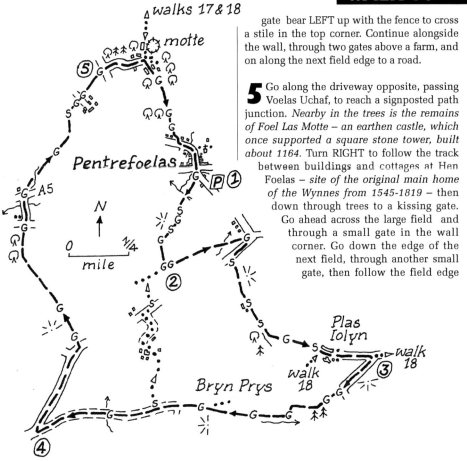

walks 17&18

motte

Pentrefoelas

A5

N

0   ¼   mile

Pentrefoelas

②

Bryn Prys

Plas Iolyn

walk 18

walk 18

③

④

gate bear LEFT up with the fence to cross a stile in the top corner. Continue alongside the wall, through two gates above a farm, and on along the next field edge to a road.

5 Go along the driveway opposite, passing Voelas Uchaf, to reach a signposted path junction. *Nearby in the trees is the remains of Foel Las Motte – an earthen castle, which once supported a square stone tower, built about 1164.* Turn RIGHT to follow the track between buildings and cottages at Hen Foelas – *site of the original main home of the Wynnes from 1545-1819* – then down through trees to a kissing gate. Go ahead across the large field and through a small gate in the wall corner. Go down the edge of the next field, through another small gate, then follow the field edge

access track to the road. Turn right, then left along a track to rejoin your outward route.)

4 Eventually you reach a road. Follow it RIGHT for about ⅓ mile. About 80 yards beyond the entrance to Gwernhywel-ganol, at a fence corner, turn LEFT off the road down to an old iron gate. Follow an old walled green track, through a gate and on across upland pasture, then on a long grad-ual descent to another gate at a lane/track junction. Continue down the lane to the A5 by a house. Cross the road with care to take the signposted path through a gate. Go up the left bank of a stream. Cross it near an old gateway and continue up the field to the left of a reedy gully to go through a gate in the corner. Walk up the field edge and at a facing

round to pass between a large bungalow and a house to the road in Pentrefoelas. Follow it LEFT through the village to the A5 by the Foelas Arms Hotel. Cross the road back to the start.

Foelas Arms Hotel

29

FOEL LAS MOTTE & FFRIDD-Y-FOEL

DESCRIPTION A 5½ mile figure of eight walk (A) through the varied countryside of the Voelas estate. The route passes an old earthwork castle, before following a lane and green track up to the edge of moorland, reaching a height of just over 1100 feet. It then follows an old drovers' road around the slopes of Ffridd-y-foel, passing an interesting example of estate enterprise, before returning on a choice of routes. Allow about 3 hours. The route can easily be shortened to a 2 mile walk (B), or extended on a good track with open views across moorland to the remote but attractive Llyn Alwen, adding 4 miles to the distance. (See **Walk 19** map).
START Car park, Pentrefoelas [SH 874 514] See **Walk 16.**

I Return to the A5 and take the road opposite from the Foelas Arms Hotel through the village, soon bending over the river and passing an old cast iron water pump. Just beyond the old school, turn RIGHT on a path signposted 'Foel Las Motte' passing between dwellings to enter a field. Bear LEFT to follow the field edge up to a small gate in the corner. Go up the next field edge, through another small gate, then continue ahead across the large field to go through a kissing-gate into the wood. Follow a stony track up through the trees, then between buildings at Hen Voelas to reach a signposted path junction. *Only a small altered cottage remains of the original cluster of buildings of Hen Voelas (Old Voelas) – the original main home of the Wynnes from 1545-1819. Voelas Hall, just over a mile to the west, became the estate home.* Continue ahead on the Mynydd Hiraethog trail through the wood. *Up to your right is the tree-topped mound of Foel Las Motte. Reputedly made by Owain Gwynedd about 1164, this tall earth castle once supported a square stone tower. Its use ceased in 1185. On your left is a large rectangular pool, which provided water for Pentrefoelas Mill.* After a gate go along the field edge to

reach a lane. (For **Walk B** turn left to point **7.**)

2 Turn RIGHT and follow the lane, as it rises steadily up the hillside. After about ½ mile, just after passing over a cattle-grid, turn LEFT on the signposted Mynydd Hiraethog trail along a track. Follow it past a small wood and on up to go through a gate into open upland country. *Pause to enjoy the extensive views of Snowdonia.* Across the valley to the north note the large walled enclosure, which you pass later. Continue up the track, passing through two further gates, to reach a signposted crossroad of paths at the edge of moorland. (For the Llyn Alwen extension, which I recommend, follow the track ahead for 2 miles across moorland, and return the same way.)

3 Leave the Mynydd Hiraethog trail by turning LEFT. Follow the path through a reedy area to the right of an old boundary and stream, soon joining a green track – *the remains of a drovers' road.* It gently descends to ford a stream by a wall/fence. *Upstream is a small waterfall.* Continue up the track to go through a gate at the corner of the large walled enclosure seen earlier. Continue along the track. *The high wall is a fine example of dry stone walling. One can only marvel at the skill, patience and time consuming effort that went into its construction in such a wild and inhospitable environment, exposed to the elements. The wall is superior in quality to others nearby. But why? A door midway deepens the mystery. A farmer later told me that the enclosure is known as 'The Warren'. It was built for hare-breeding by Voelas estate, presumably at a time when jugged, roast, boiled, potted and hashed hare were culinary delights!*

4 After going through a gate at the far end of the enclosure follow the track alongside the wall – *enjoying a panorama of mountains from Arenig to the northern Carneddau. Cattle still graze the upland pastures – a reminder of times gone by when animals were fattened on these slopes before being taken by drovers to distant markets.* After a gate, the track descends and passes

Ffridd-y-Foel

N

0   ¼   mile

to
Llyn Alwen

walks 18 & 19

Maes Gwyn

Foel Las Motte

walk 16

Pentrefoelas   A5

P

walks 16 & 18

choice. For the main route bear LEFT along a green track to a gate, then follow the track down to pass through a farm and follow its access track to reach the lane. Follow it RIGHT. (An alternative option is to bear right past the house and go through a gate on the left just beyond into a field. Go half-right down the field to go through a gate near the bottom corner. Turn right along the field edge, then bear left to cross an old gate and stepping stones over a river. Keep ahead on the line of an old track through a reedy area, soon bearing left along a clearer track to the road by a house. Follow it down to point **6**.)

6 At a road junction, a short detour RIGHT will bring you to a fine stone arched bridge over the river and nearby Maes Gwyn dating from 1665. Return along the road and follow it towards Pentrefoelas. Shortly, turn LEFT along a driveway to go past Voelas Uchaf to the signposted path junction at Hen Voelas. Turn RIGHT and return along your outward route, or continue on the road back to the village, passing the former keeper's cottage.

through another gate. Just beyond go through a gate on the left and descend a walled track towards a farm. After going through a gate at the bottom, immediately go through another gate on the left. Go alongside the wall above the farmhouse and through a gate in it. Continue with the wall on your left to pass through a gate in the corner. Now head down the field to go through a gate near the right-hand corner. Keep ahead across the mid-slope of the next field above telegraph poles to go through a gate on a track. Continue along the track.

5 At a waymarked path junction by the outbuilding of a house you have a

Water pump

31

WALK 18
THE PENTREFOELAS ROUND

DESCRIPTION A 7½ mile walk (**A**) or shorter 4½ mile walk (**B**), using paths, old coaching and drovers' routes and quiet lanes, through open countryside around Pentrefoelas, with excellent views throughout. The route rises in stages to Bryn Prys at just over 1000 feet before descending to pass an historical house, then continuing to the hamlet of Rhydlydan, with its country inn. It then meanders north to skirt moorland, reaching over 1100 feet, before descending to Pentrefoelas. Allow about 4½ hours.
START Car park, Pentrefoelas [SH 874 514] See **Walk 16.**

1 Follow instructions in the first section of **Walk 16.**

2 Turn RIGHT along a green track – *part of the original late 18thC London-Holyhead coach road*. At a track junction, follow the track LEFT to a road. Turn RIGHT and after 100 yards, go LEFT up a stony track to follow a waymarked path through Gallt-y-celyn farm. Continue up a green track, soon becoming enclosed to cross a stile onto a stony track. Turn LEFT along the track and, when it bends right, continue ahead on a green track – *an old drovers' route.*

3 Shortly after going through a gate, cross a waymarked stile on the left and the wall ahead. Now angle up the nearby lower gorse covered slope of Bryn Prys, and on in the same direction to cross the bend of a green track. Continue past the edge of a small plantation, crossing a reedy area. Go past the plantation corner and on to go through a gate in the wall ahead. Go onto the small ridge to enjoy the panoramic views. Descend the slope towards the right hand corner of the forest below, to join a green track. Follow it to pass through a second gate by the corner of another small plantation. Go ahead

towards the stone 'Great Barn' of Plas Iolyn, turn LEFT through another gate, then bear RIGHT to pass between outbuildings and the house. Follow its driveway to a minor road.(See **Walk 15** for information on Plas Iolyn.) Follow the road ahead – *a continuation of the earlier drovers' route* – over a crossroad – *the line of a Roman road from Bala to Conwy* – and on to reach a junction at Rhydlydan. Turn LEFT to the Giler Arms Hotel, where refreshments are available. *Nearby, in 1820, during construction of Telford's new road (the A5) 40 longcist graves were uncovered and a 5th/6th C inscribed stone found. It commemorated Brohomaglus Iattus and his wife Caune, and indicated links with Christians in southern Gaul.*

4 Continue along the road – *a section of the old London–Holyhead coach road that Telford's road replaced* – to descend to a junction by a 19thC chapel. Here, turn RIGHT along the access track to Pentre Felin. Pass in front of the house to go through a gate. Immediately turn RIGHT to pass to the left of stone outbuildings, then descend to a footbridge over the river and continue up to the A5. Cross the road with care and the stile opposite. Go up the edge of a reedy field, through a field gap, and then a gate into the old farmyard of Cefngarw. (For **Walk B** go left and follow an enclosed green track to the A543. Cross the road and follow it left, then take a signposted path on the right to pass between a cluster of buildings and on across fields to Pentrefoelas.)

5 For the main route turn RIGHT and follow an old green track for ⅓ mile to a gate by a cottage. Follow its access track to the bend of a road. Continue ahead, and at a junction, turn LEFT and follow the road past a cottage to cross a footbridge over a river. At the next junction, follow the road LEFT to the A543. Turn RIGHT along the road, then turn LEFT up a lane past a cottage and bungalow. When it bends towards a farm, continue up a waymarked enclosed green track. After going through a gate, bend RIGHT up a wider enclosed track. *Like the one just left, this is an old drovers' route used to move* *animals to markets in Denbigh and further afield in Cheshire and Shropshire.* After going through a set of gates at its end, continue with the line of the old green track alongside the boundary as it contours the slopes of Cefnen Wen, passing through further gates. Eventually it descends gently to a crossroad of tracks by a finger post

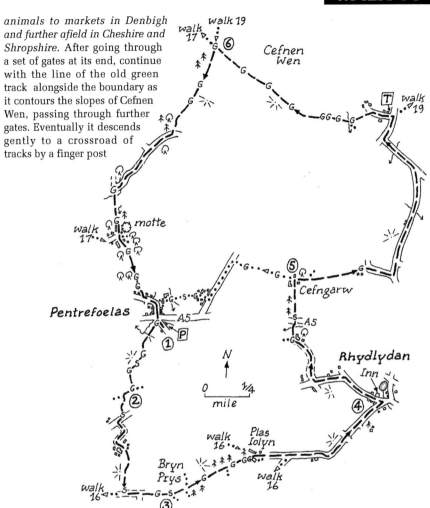

6 Turn LEFT through the gate and follow a delightful gated green track down to a lane. Follow it RIGHT for about ½ mile on a steady descent. Just before a cattle grid, go through a kissing gate on the left. Walk along the field edge and through a wood past a small reservoir. *Up to your left is tree-topped mound of Foel Las Motte, which once supported a square stone tower, built about 1164.* At a finger post continue on the track ahead to pass between buildings and cot-

tages at Hen Foelas – *site of the original main home of the Wynnes from 1545-1819* – then down through trees to a kissing gate. Go ahead across the large field and through a small gate in the wall corner. Go down the field edge, through another small gate, then follow the field edge round to pass between a large bungalow and a house to the road in Pentrefoelas. Follow it LEFT through the village to the A5 by the Foelas Arms Hotel, where refreshments are available.

THE THREE LAKES TRAIL

DESCRIPTION An exhilarating 10½ mile moorland walk in the heart of Mynydd Hiraethog, visiting three upland lakes of different character – Llyn Aled, the remote natural lake of Llyn Alwen, and the Alwen reservoir. This route requires careful navigation at times and is for the experienced well equipped walker who likes wild open moorland. It is best undertaken on a clear sunny day, when the treeless landscape is magical and the panoramic views superb. The initial section to Llyn Alwen is the most demanding, crossing largely pathless and sometimes boggy moorland. It is then followed by a superb 2 mile green track across remote moorland, then an old drovers' route. The return follows the route of a medieval road up Bwlch y Garnedd and down to cross the Alwen reservoir for an easy final section along bridleways and road. Allow about 5½ – 6 hours.

START The dam, Llyn Aled. [SH 916579]

DIRECTIONS From the A543 Denbigh-Pentrefoelas road take the minor road signposted to Llyn Aled to park by the lake just before it crosses the dam.

1 Follow instructions in the first section of **Walk 20**.

2 Descend through a reedy area and continue up to the inauspicious top of Moel Llyn ahead. Now go half-LEFT down towards the tops of two trees near the right hand end of Llyn Alwen, soon joining a steadily improving path. When it splits take the RIGHT fork, then bear RIGHT around a depression and on past a red-topped post. Descend via a gate to the old farm of Ty'n-llyn below. *This idyllic location beside the hidden beauty of this remote lake, surrounded by wild and inhospitable moorland makes a gem of a stop on a fine day – a haven of peace and tranquility.* Leave the farm by its green access track alongside the lake edge. After going through a gate you quickly leave

the lake behind to follow the delightful green track for 2 miles across the expansive wild moorland. *After the earlier rough crossing it is a pleasure to stride out on this safe passage through such a wild landscape, enjoying the extensive views.* After going through a second gate *there are good views of Moel Hebog, the Nantlle ridge, Snowdon, the Glyders, Tryfan and the Carneddau.* Eventually the track reaches a signposted crossroad of paths at a track junction just before a gate.

3 Turn LEFT on the waymarked Mynydd Hiraethog trail and follow an old gated green track – *variable in quality* – alongside a wall, contouring the mid-slopes of Cefnen Wen. *This is an old drovers' route used to move animals to markets in Denbigh and further afield in Cheshire and Shropshire.* After a double set of gates, the track becomes enclosed and begins to descend. About 150 yards after passing through another gate, at the broadest section of the track, bear LEFT through a waymarked gate. Now follow another enclosed track to descend past a farm, and continue down its access lane to the A543. Go through the waymarked gate opposite, then go half-LEFT to cross a footbridge over a stream. Continue up the slope ahead to follow a wide enclosed track past farm buildings to go through a second gate into open country.

4 Continue ahead alongside the old wall to join and follow an enclosed track, soon bending half-LEFT. After going through a gate, keep with this delightful, but steadily deteriorating track, as it rises gently across open upland pasture. Go through a gate just above the track and continue ahead to pass a small ruin. Continue along the line of the old track. *Note the many lichen-covered stones.* At a more distinct cross track, turn RIGHT and soon follow the line of the old embanked Pentrefoelas-Denbigh road rising up Bwlch y Garnedd. *This ancient road fell out of use after the building of the turnpike road, now the A543, in 1826.* After passing a large squat stone, continue with a clear path along the right side of the old road to reach the top of the bwlch. *Up to the right is the cairned top of heather covered Mwdwl-eithin. A boul-*

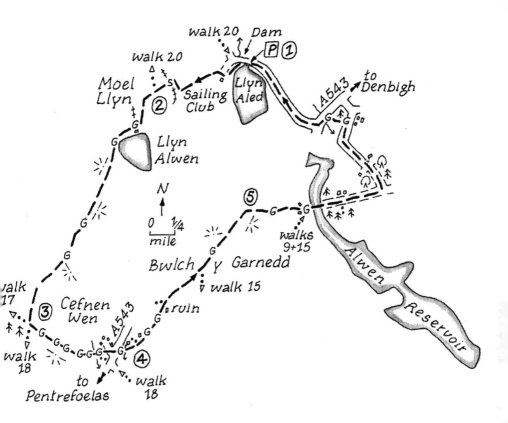

der near the top of the pass makes a good place for a break to enjoy the views, soon to disappear. *From the top of the bwlch can be seen Llyn Aled and Llyn Alwen.* Follow a path across the reedy moorland, where little remains of the old road, to go through a gate in the fence ahead. Continue on the line of the old track as it contours north east across tussocky/reedy ground.

5 At a good view of Alwen reservoir, the old track goes half-RIGHT and descends to a gate, then continues down the hillside – *enjoying panoramic views of Alwen reservoir en route – to reach a tree by the small ruin of Nant Heilyn – the former home of Heilyn, an 18thC highwayman, whose hoard of stolen silver and gold may still lie hidden nearby!*

Go past nearby sheepfolds to join the Alwen trail path at a bridge over the stream. Follow it to cross a long footbridge over the neck of the reservoir. Continue up a stony track (a bridleway) past the house of Pen-y-ffrith, and keep with the track for about ½ mile. At a signposted bridleway junction, turn LEFT along another track, shortly descending past the entrance to Hafod Elwy Hall and the large stone outbuilding of Tan-y-graig farm. Continue with the access track, then at the next farm, go through a gate on the left opposite a barn. Go past a small plantation and follow the fence round to a gate above a stream to reach the A543. Cross the road and follow it LEFT, then take the road back to Llyn Aled. The expansive beauty of the lake makes an enjoyable finale to the walk.

WALK 20

AROUND ALED ISAF

DESCRIPTION A 8½ mile (A) or 7½ mile walk (B) exploring the expansive tract of moorland and upland pasture in the northern part of Mynydd Hiraethog near the upland lakes of Llyn Aled and Isaf Aled, offering extensive views. The route crosses moorland just west of Llyn Aled, before heading north across a moorland plateau. The main route (A) follows a delightful upland track via Llys Dymper, while route (B) continues north through moorland/pastureland. Both routes return across the moorland top of Foel Lwyd, then follow an attractive upland road, passing by a gorge and Rhaeadr y Bedd waterfall, and on alongside Aled Isaf. This route is for the experienced walker, for its outward route crosses wild moorland, boggy in parts, that requires careful navigation. It should be avoided in poor visibility. Allow about 4½ hours. A less demanding shorter 5 mile walk can be created by combining Routes A and B, starting from limited vergeside parking on the lane leading to point 5.

START The dam, Llyn Aled [SH 916579]

DIRECTIONS From the A543 Denbigh-Pentrefoelas road take the minor road signposted to Llyn Aled to park by the lake just before it crosses the dam.

I From the castellated stone building that controls the outflow from Llyn Aled, built in 1934 as a regulating reservoir, walk along the reedy edge of the lake towards the sailing club, crossing a stream and a fence. At the slipway bear RIGHT to cross a stile by the sailing club's access gate/track. Go up a green track ahead. It soon bends LEFT and ends after about 100 yards. Continue straight ahead, and after a few yards, take the right fork of a path. It heads across moorland along the left hand edge of a shallow valley, passing on the higher ground to your right, a descending tree/hedge boundary, then a small stone sheepfold. At the slight head of the valley, leave the path, which bends left, and continue straight ahead. Work your

way across the right hand side of an expanse of boggy moorland to reach a fence near its corner, where stands an old inscribed slate boundary stone. Turn RIGHT and walk alongside the fence, rising gently to cross an old stile in the fence on a small ridge, after a few hundred yards. Now go up onto the top of the ridge to enjoy the extensive views – *south east over Llyn Aled to Clocaenog Forest; south to Alwen reservoir and the distant Berwyns; south west a glimpse of Llyn Alwen and the distant Arans, Arenig and Rhinogs; to the north west the Carneddau range and Tryfan. To the east on the skyline is the ruin of Gwylfa Hiraethog (details in* **Walk 7**). Walk along its broad top.

2 After about 200 yards swing sharp RIGHT across the moorland plateau – to cross an old gate in the fence, about 150 yards beyond another boundary stone. Continue straight ahead northwards across the wide expanse of moorland, aiming for the eastern end of a distant green ridge. After a few hundred yards, you will pick up a clear path, with drier conditions underfoot. Soon the path parallels a fence on your left. After crossing a stream near the fence, go up the slope ahead and past sheepfolds. Follow the fence down to a gate in the corner

3 Here you have a choice. (For **Route B**, continue initially alongside the fence, then head down across reedy ground towards distant small plantations, to cross an old gate in the corner. Follow an old boundary embankment ahead, over a stream and on to cross a stock gate at its end. Follow the fenced embankment on your right. At its corner, continue up the slope ahead and across the small flat tussocky hilltop of Bryn Poeth. As you begin a gentle descent, cross stile in the fence on your left. Go half-right, through a gate and on down the middle of a long field to a gate. Continue down the next field past a small gorge and pool to a stile. Descend through gorse to a track to reach a lane at point 5.) For **Route A**, go through the gate and another just ahead, then follow a delightful green track up to a gate and on across the grassy ridge of Llys Dymper. At a track junction – *with extensive views* across to the Snowdonia mountains and prominent wind turbines – bear RIGHT and continue along this delightful level upland gated track.

4 After about 1 mile, the track begins a long steady descent – *with views of the coastal windfarm* – later levelling out, passing a derelict cottage and becoming a lane. Follow it down to take a signposted over a stile on the right. Walk ahead down the field to cross a gate below a derelict cottage. After going through another gate, bear RIGHT along a green track, which rises to a gate. The track now rises steadily across the edge of reedy terrain alongside a stream. After a gate, continue ahead near the stream, over another, and on along the field edge, past sheepfolds, then follow a green track to a gate onto a lane

5 Follow the lane RIGHT past Tynyffynnon, then take the signposted path up the access track to Tai'n-y-foel. Go through a gate on the right, then continue up the field edge to a gate in the corner. Keep straight ahead, soon on a faint green track to cross the wide moorland top of Foel Lwyd and then descend alongside a fence. At its corner, bend LEFT through a reedy area to reach the road by a ruined cottage. Turn RIGHT along the road, soon descending to cross the dam of Aled Isaf – *a regulating reservoir built in the 1930s – by an impressive gorge containing Rhaeadr y Bedd waterfall. During 1974, low water levels revealed flint artefacts and other evidence on the reservoir bed of occupation by mesolithic hunter/gatherers, who roamed through this area when a gentler climate and woodland habitat made it a less hostile environment. Continue with the road alongside the lake and on back to Llyn Aled.*

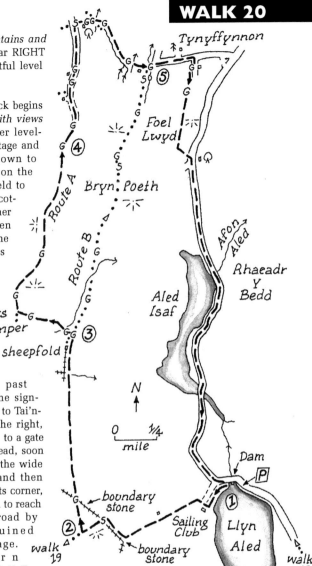

Boundary stone

WALK 21

AROUND CWM CLEDWEN

DESCRIPTION A 6-mile walk (**A**) exploring the hills on both sides of the Cledwen valley in which lies the remote ancient community of Gwytherin. It offers extensive views, especially of the Snowdonia mountains. The route rises steadily to reach upland pasture at over 1200 feet, before descending back into Cwm Cledwen. It then climbs an attractive side valley and crosses an expansive moorland plateau, reaching a height of over 1300 feet, before descending to the Lion Inn (*01745 860123 for opening times*) in Gwytherin. Allow about 4 hours. By utilising the quiet valley road, the route can easily be undertaken as two separate walks of 4 (**B**) and 4½ (**C**) miles.

START Gwytherin [SH 876615]

DIRECTIONS Gwytherin lies 4 miles south west of Llansannan on the B5384. Park tidily in the village.

*G*wytherin is a remote community, with an important ecclesiastical past. The church, dedicated to St. Winifred, was built in 1869 to replace an earlier one. Legend has it that St. Winifred, associated with the 'holy well' in Holywell, later came to Gwytherin, where she became abbess at a local nunnery in the 12thC. After her death her remains were kept in the former church, but were eventually transferred to Shrewsbury. The churchyard contains old yew trees, and on the north side of the church stand a line of 4 small standing stones. One, dating from the 5th-6thC and inscribed in Latin, commemorates Vinne-maglus. Such stones provided the earliest evidence of Christianity. In the village centre on the site of a former smithy is a plaque to one of its famous sons, Clwydfardd (1800–94), the first Archdruid.

I (For **Walk C** follow the road south to point 3.) At the village T-junction, turn RIGHT (the B5384) past the post box. Take the 'No through road' on the right, past the community centre, over the Afon Cledwen

and on through a cluster of farm buildings. Continue along the lane to its end at another farm. Here bear LEFT past a stone outbuilding, through a gate and on up a concrete track, soon becoming stony and continuing to rise steadily. After a gate, where it briefly levels out, the stony track bears LEFT through another gate and climbs the hillside, later levelling out.

2 When the track heads half-left, go through a gate ahead. Go across upland pasture and through a gate in the fence ahead. Keep ahead past a reedy area, then go through a gate in the embanked fence boundary. Bear RIGHT to follow a gully/stream down to the end of a ruined cottage. Cross the stream and go through a small gate in the fence, then go across the slope to join a green track, passing through two gates by a sheepfold. The track heads west – *with views south into the heart of Mynydd Hiraethog.* Shortly, at a track junction, bear LEFT down to go through a gate. Leave the track and go half-RIGHT to descend a short old sunken green track. Go over a cross-track and on to a gate in the fence ahead. Go across the next field, parallel with the fence on your right, towards the panorama of mountains – *Moel Siabod, Snowdon, the Glyders, Tryfan, and the Carneddau range.* After about 250 yards, bear LEFT to join a faint green track beneath a small knoll to go through a gateway in the fence. Continue ahead, soon descending more steeply the hillside to go through a gate in the fence corner. Now follow a green track down alongside the old field embankment. It meanders down the hillside to eventually ford a stream and continues past a footbridge to a farm. Cross a ladder-stile by the first building, then follow the field edge past the farm to cross a stile in the corner and a footbridge over the river. Turn RIGHT along the road for ¼ mile.

3 Turn up the access track to Tai Pella. (For **Walk B** follow the road back along the valley). After passing the first large barn, turn RIGHT and go through a gate by a stream. Now follow a stony track up the attractive side valley. After ⅓ mile, where a fork of the track does a sharp U-turn on the right, keep

38

ahead to cross a confluence of streams, then follow the track LEFT up the slope, and on up the left hand side of the narrow valley. After a gate, the track continues up the reedy terrain to a road. Follow it RIGHT, and after about 300 yards go through a gate on your left opposite another (or follow the road down to Gwytherin). Go across upland pasture towards wind turbines and through a gate in the fence ahead, at a fence corner just to the right of a reedy area Angle LEFT through reeds and across pasture, soon descending to go through more reeds to cross a waymarked stile in a fence corner. Now follow the fence on your left, rising gently across moorland – *enjoying extensive views* – to eventually go through a gate. Continue beside the fence.

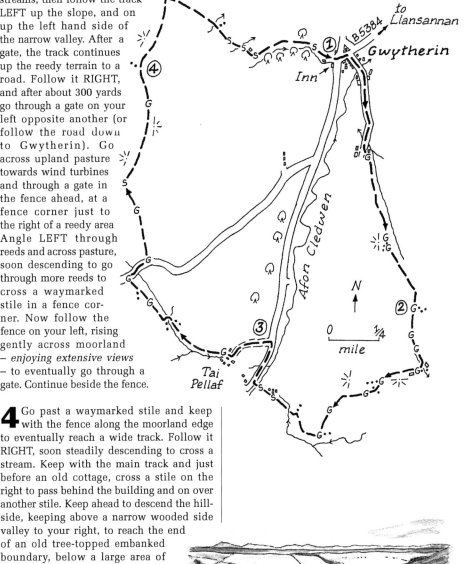

4 Go past a waymarked stile and keep with the fence along the moorland edge to eventually reach a wide track. Follow it RIGHT, soon steadily descending to cross a stream. Keep with the main track and just before an old cottage, cross a stile on the right to pass behind the building and on over another stile. Keep ahead to descend the hillside, keeping above a narrow wooded side valley to your right, to reach the end of an old tree-topped embanked boundary, below a large area of gorse. Descend through the trees, with the boundary on your left, then follow a clear path down the edge of the wooded valley, moving steadily closer to the stream below. Cross a stile and follow the stream down to pass a house and on to reach the road by the Lion Inn.

View towards the mountains of Snowdonia

PRONUNCIATION

These basic points should help non-Welsh speakers

Welsh	English equivalent
c	always hard, as in cat
ch	as in the Scottish word loch
dd	as th in then
f	as v in vocal
ff	as f
g	always hard as in got
ll	no real equivalent. It is like 'th' in then, but with an 'L' sound added to it, giving 'thlan' for the pronunciation of the Welsh 'Llan'.

In Welsh the accent usually falls on the last-but-one syllable of a word.

KEY TO THE MAPS

- ➡ Walk route and direction
- ═ Metalled road
- ‒‒‒ Unsurfaced road
- •••• Footpath/route adjoining walk route
- ∿ River/stream
- ♣ ♫ Trees
- ▬■ Railway
- **G** Gate
- **S** Stile
- **F.B.** Footbridge
- ⊻ Viewpoint
- P Parking
- T Telephone
- ⌂ Caravan site

THE COUNTRY CODE

- Be safe – plan ahead and follow any signs
- Leave gates and property as you find them
- Protect plants and animals, and take your litter home
- Keep dogs under close control
- Consider other people

The CRoW Act 2000, implemented throughout Wales in May 2005, introduced new legal rights of access for walkers to designated open country, predominantly mountain, moor, heath or down, plus all registered common land. This access can be subject to restrictions and closure for land management or safety reasons for up to 28 days a year. The following web site operated by Countryside Council for Wales will provide updated information on any closures.
www.ccw.gov.uk

Published by
Kittiwake
3 Glantwymyn Village Workshops, Glantwymyn, Machynlleth, Montgomeryshire SY20 8LY

© Text & map research: David Berry 2007
© Maps & illustrations: Kittiwake 2007
Illustrations by Morag Perrott
Cover photographs: David Berry – large: View across Cwm Merddwr (Walk 14); inset: Bagot's Monument, Pincyn Llys (Walks 3 & 4)

Care has been taken to be accurate. However neither the author nor the publisher can accept responsibility for any errors which may appear, or their consequences. If you are in doubt about any path, check before you start out.

Printed by MWL, Pontpool

ISBN: 978 1 902302 53 9